THEATRE ARTS 2

Student Handbook

On-Stage and Off-Stage Roles:
Fitting the Pieces Together

SECOND EDITION

ALAN ENGELSMAN
AND
PENNY ENGELSMAN

MERIWETHER PUBLISHING LTD.
Colorado Springs, Colorado

Meriwether Publishing Ltd., Publisher
P.O. Box 7710
Colorado Springs, CO 80933

Editorial coordinator: Amber Crawford
Typesetting: Sharon E. Garlock
Cover and book design: Janice Melvin

Library of Congress Cataloging-in-Publication Data

Engelsman, Alan, 1932-
    Theatre arts 2 student handbook : on-stage and off-stage roles: fitting the pieces together / by Alan Engelsman and Penny Engelsman. -- 2nd ed.
        p.   cm.
            Summary: Presents units on many aspects of theater, including playwriting, monologues, puppetry, set design, theater business, makeup, acting, directing, and theater history.
        ISBN 1-56608-040-1 (pbk.)
        1. College and school drama. 2. Amateur theater--Production and direction. 3. Young adult drama, American. [1. Theater--Production and direction.]   I. Engelsman, Penny, 1943-
II. Title.
PN3175.E55   1998
792--dc21

                                                                      98-10438
                                                                         CIP
                                                                          AC

2   3   4   5   6   7   00   01   02   03

We dedicate this new *Theatre Arts 2 Student Handbook* to *you,* the student. You possess enthusiasm, intelligence, a multitude of skills, humor, energy, and our hope for a better tomorrow. We know that you will succeed in each activity in this text. We believe in you and we are proud of you — now — and throughout your life.

We also dedicate this textbook to Julie Rae and Jeff, who still love Halloween, costumes and makeup. May they cherish the memories of the plays in the backyard. And may they never forget to take the time to create some theatre magic in their own lives.

ACKNOWLEDGMENTS

Grateful acknowledgment is made to the publishers, authors, or copyright holders for permission to use the following materials in this book:

The Theatre Cube design is used by permission of Thomas Beagle, Antioch, California.

The "Theatre Class Evaluation Form," developed by Rosalind M. Flynn and described in an AATSE journal article titled "A Performance Evaluation That Works," is used by permission of Gerald Ratliff, editor of the *American Association for Theatre in Secondary Education Journal*, Winter, 1987.

"Horace and Alphonse" by Penny Engelsman, copyright © 1997, is reprinted by permission of Alpen & Jeffries Publishers.

"The Old Man and His Affectionate Son" is reprinted from *Folk Tales of Old Japan,* published by The Japan Times, Ltd., Tokyo, Japan. Copyright © 1975 by the Japan Times, Ltd.

The authors also wish to acknowledge technical advice offered by Jim Burwinkel, Janet Keifer, Don Jones, Christine Murray, Ginny Weiss and Baron Winchester.

Graphics for this book were designed by Alan and Penny Engelsman, David Jourden and Janice Melvin.

NOTE

In this text the authors have frequently used the pronoun phrase "he or she." It is their way of acknowledging that student actors, directors or designers may be male or female. The same phrase is used in reference to instructors. Sometimes, however, sentences containing the phrase "he or she" sound awkward or wordy. In those instances, the authors have chosen to use only "she" or only "he" with the belief that the reader will understand that no sexist stereotyping is intended.

Contents

WELCOME
To the Student

The *Theatre Arts 2 Student Handbook* is different from other textbooks. We do not expect you to read long chapters and then write answers to lengthy questions at home. Rather, each unit of the *Theatre Arts 2 Student Handbook* provides opportunities for you to do something other than just sit and listen to a lecture. Students will work on teams and participate in activities. Often you will create objects relating to theatre. At other times, you will learn about makeup by creating scars, bruises, cuts and black eyes. You will learn to outline a play in thirty minutes by playing "The Playwriting Game: Storyboard," and your entire class will make puppets and give a puppet show.

The full title of this textbook is *Theatre Arts 2 Student Handbook – On-Stage and Off-Stage Roles: Fitting the Pieces Together*. You will be reminded throughout this text of the collaborative nature of theatre. "Collaborate" means to work together. The word "collaborate" is similar to the word "cooperate." Both words stress the idea that each person depends on everyone else in the group in order to be successful.

Everyone is equal. No one person is more important than anyone else. A theatre group is similar to an orchestra. When everyone plays his or her instruments at the same time and when everyone plays his notes properly, the music sounds harmonious. In theatre when everyone does his job in harmony with the rest of the group, everyone experiences success. Have a wonderful semester and enjoy each of the units in the *Theatre Arts 2 Student Handbook*. We know you will be successful!

The Theatre Cube

Do you remember the first play you were in? Was it in grade school? Was it an informal play in the classroom? Or was it a high school play? What do you remember most about the experience?

Did you have to wear special clothing? Did someone help you with your "costume" by giving you a hat or scarf? Did anyone else offer to bring the "props," like a bat and ball or fake fruit or a cup and saucer? Did your teacher work with each actor on the spoken parts?

It does not matter whether you remember a small play in the classroom, a holiday play in the auditorium, or a full-length play in the high school. Each of you had a similar experience. You learned to work as part of a team. You learned that theatre requires the efforts of many individuals: directors, props personnel, set designers, actors, makeup artists and costumers.

ACTIVITY #1

What Is a "Collaborative" Art?

Theatre, dance and music are performing arts. They differ from arts like painting, writing, and sculpting. The performing arts require the cooperation of artists with specialized talents. Many artists are involved in a production:

the playwright	the set designer
the actors	the lighting designer
the director	the makeup artist
the composer and	the costume designer
musicians (when	the choreographer
music is involved)	(when dance is involved)

The performing arts require the cooperation of artists with specialized talents.

Every team member is important. Actors sometimes think that they are the most important people in a company. But they soon discover that they are just part of a team.

The various artists are supported by the stage manager, the prop master, set builders, scenery painters, spotlight operators and box office personnel. The list seems to grow and grow. When you next attend a play, read the program carefully. You will find that more people are working behind the scenes than on the stage. Acting is only a part of theatre.

Purpose of Activity #1

After reading and discussing the information in Activity #1, students will begin to understand the collaborative nature of theatre.

DIRECTIONS

1. Read aloud paragraphs A, B and C.

2. Using a dictionary, look up the word "collaborate." Next, look up the word "cooperate." Last, look at the definitions for all the words that begin with the letters "cooper" and "coordin." One of the definitions for all of these words is "of equal order, rank or importance." What does this mean? How might this definition apply to theatre? Another definition for a word with the letters "coordin" is "harmonious action." What does harmonious mean? How can you apply this word to theatre?

A. *The Theatre Arts 2 Student Handbook* examines the various roles people play in creating theatre. While participating in each new activity, you may find new ways in which you can contribute to theatre. You may discover roles that excite you even more than acting.

B. In each unit you will work as part of a team. You will learn to write short plays, tell stories, perform monologs, design ground plans, use stage makeup, give a puppet play, design a play program, create a production budget and participate in an end-of-semester production.

C. You will learn to do each of these activities as a member of a team. Your team will ensure that everyone in that group succeeds. Everyone will assist other team members with assignments and activities. Students are evaluated on their team efforts, not just their individual performance. A team is successful only if each member succeeds. Team members quickly learn the collaborative nature of theatre. In each unit you will apply the principles of the Theatre Cube model.

ACTIVITY #2

What Is a Theatre Cube Model?

Purpose of Activity #2

After reading and discussing the information in Activity #2, students will begin to understand the concept of a Theatre Cube model.

DIRECTIONS

1. Read aloud paragraphs A, B and C.

2. Answer the following questions: (a) What is a Theatre Cube model? (b) What is a "conceptual model"? (c) Can you give an example of a conceptual model? (d) Why would someone create a conceptual model? (e) You are only able to see three illustrations in this Theatre Cube model. Are there other pictures not shown on the other sides of the cube? (f) Who created the Theatre Cube model?

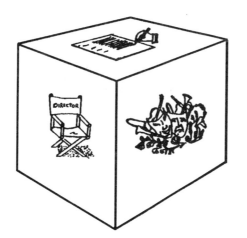

Activity #2 — Illustration 1

Every person combines his talents and ideas with those of others in order to create a successful product.

A. Unit One concentrates on the collaborative nature of theatre. The word "collaborative" is similar in meaning to the word "cooperative." Every person combines his talents and ideas with those of others in order to create a successful product. The Theatre Cube model and the following activities were originally developed by a high school teacher named Thomas Beagle. The Theatre Cube model is an artistic representation of this *interaction* of talented people.

B. When people see the word "model," they usually imagine a smaller version of an object: a model car, plane, or a model set. Some models, however, are not miniature copies of an object or setting. Instead, they are large models. These models represent a concept or idea. They are called *conceptual* models. Have you ever seen a model of a molecule? It is an example of a conceptual model.

Activity #2 — Illustration 2

C. The conceptual model in Illustration 2 helps us to understand the way in which atoms are connected and held together. The Theatre Cube is another conceptual model. It illustrates the connected, cooperative nature of all theatre artists and theatre contributors.

ACTIVITY #3

Creating the Six-Sided Theatre Cube

In Activity #3 you will create your own theatre cube. When you hold your completed cube in your hand, you will see how the six sides of the cube are interconnected. You will begin to understand the collaborative nature of theatre.

Purpose of Activity #3

The cube illustrates the interconnected nature of theatre.

Each class member will create a paper cube. The cube illustrates the interconnected nature of theatre.

Your instructor will give you a sheet of paper on which you will find a design. There also will be instructions explaining how to cut, fold and tape the paper so that it forms a cube. Every student will make a cube. Prepare the paper for assembly. However, do not tape it together yet. Read the following directions before finishing your cube.

DIRECTIONS

1. Note that the four center squares are labeled: Side #1, Side #2, Side #3, Side #4, respectively.

   a. Below the picture on Side #1 write the word DIRECTING.

   b. Below the picture on Side #2 write the word ACTING.

   c. Below the picture on Side #3 write the word DESIGNING.

   d. Below the picture on Side #4 write the word BUSINESS.

2. Note that two other squares have labels: Side #5 and Side #6.

   a. Below the picture on Side #5 write the word PLAYWRITING. Below that word, write you own name.

   b. Below the picture on Side #6 write the word HISTORY.

   c. Draw arrows pointing outward on each side of the cube. Illustration 1 shows you where to place the arrows.

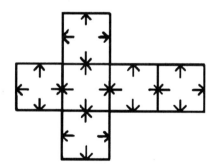

Activity #3 — Illustration 1

   d. Tape and staple your cube together. You are done.

Why did Mr. Beagle use a cube to explain theatre arts? Why didn't he use a sphere? Or a pyramid? Or a triangle?

Working in groups, try to help each other label the cube. Be prepared to discuss why you think Thomas Beagle created this cube. Why did Mr. Beagle use a cube to explain theatre arts? Why didn't he use a sphere? Or a pyramid? Or a triangle?

ACTIVITY #4
Reading Activity

Purpose of Activity #4

Students will read sections of the passages in Activity #4 in order to understand the cooperative and connective nature of theatre.

DIRECTIONS

1. Read the following explanation aloud.

2. Discuss what you learned from these brief passages.

Hold your Theatre Cube model in your hand. Look at the top side titled PLAYWRITING. It has four arrows. Each one points to one of the four sides.

> **Both the playwright and director should have a common understanding about the purpose and theme of the play.**

There is a reason for these arrows. The playwright affects each of the four sides. Both the playwright and director should have a common understanding about the purpose and theme of the play. These two people must share their ideas. When the playwright is not present, the script should clearly reveal the author's views. Both the writer and the director depend on each other for good communication.

Dialog and stage directions in a play are important to the actor. The actor needs this information to understand the character that he or she is playing. Stage directions and dialog help actors understand a character's personality and behavior.

The playwright needs to consult closely with design and technical personnel. Scenery, lighting, sound, costumes, makeup and props make a play "come alive" on-stage. However, the writer cannot always be on the set in person to speak to the crew.

Therefore, the writer must include information in his/her script about stage directions, set designs, scenery, lighting and costumes. The writer also communicates information in the dialog of the play. By studying the play closely, the technical crew is able to create the scenery, lighting and costumes that the writer originally wanted.

Finally, the playwright must understand the money and business conditions of the production company. The budget of a company will determine what kind of sets they can build: plain or fancy. In addition, if funds are limited, a playwright might need to consider cutting some characters from the play. This change would save money on actors' salaries.

While holding the cube in your hand, look at its side panels. Note that each side has four arrows. Each of these arrows touches four other sides.

The arrow at the top of each side points to PLAYWRITING (or the playwright). The arrows suggest that directors, actors, designers and business managers will all look at a play from a different angle. Each team member has a responsibility to the play and playwright.

Each person tries to interpret the meaning and purpose of the words. However, these team members are not allowed to cut lines because of a particular need. Each assisting person may suggest slight changes (and sometimes, even major ones) to the playwright. But they should honor the author's wishes and intentions.

Each assisting person may suggest slight changes (and sometimes, even major ones) to the playwright. But they should honor the author's wishes and intentions.

The arrows on the cube's sides point to the right and left. Start with DIRECTING, Side #1. Its arrow points to the right. The arrow shows that the director has a commitment to the actors. He/she must provide leadership and encouragement. The director must also allow actors to be creative.

Note the arrow at the left side of the ACTING panel. It suggests that actors must show loyalty and respect for the director's authority. However, they should be free to make suggestions to the director. Often, their ideas will help the audience to better understand a play.

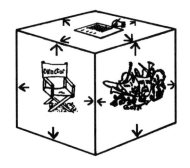

Activity #4 — Illustration 1

Return to Side #1. One arrow points to the left. It shows that the director depends on the business manager. This person advertises the play and is responsible for making a profit.

The director and business manager must work together. They need a budget for salaries, building materials and other supplies. If income does not cover expenses, the director will have to make changes in production plans.

The director and business manager must work together... If income does not cover expenses, the director will have to make changes in production plans.

Look now at the right arrow on the panel labeled BUSINESS. It suggests that the business manager must be sensitive to the director's goals. Every performance needs to have an audience. The business staff brings that audience to the theatre. They create an attractive theatre experience. The business staff is responsible for making the audience want to return to the theatre to see future plays.

In order to advertise the play well, the business manager must talk to the director. He needs to learn which parts of the production will bring an audience to the theatre.

Now you understand the arrows. They indicate that everyone depends on one another. Each person has to understand the goals and ideas of others. Everyone in theatre is important. The Theatre Cube reminds us that everyone has to work together for a successful performance.

ACTIVITY #5

Group Activity: Answering Questions About the Theatre Cube Model

Purpose of Activity #5

With the help of team members, students will answer each of the questions in Activity #5. You will better understand the collaborative nature of theatre.

DIRECTIONS

1. You will continue working with your teammates from Day One.

2. Read the following six questions aloud.

3. As a team, answer each of the following questions.

(a) How does ACTING relate to the PLAYWRIGHT?

_____

(b) How does ACTING relate to the DIRECTOR?

_____

(c) How does ACTING relate to DESIGNING?

_____

(d) How does ACTING relate to the BUSINESS side?

_____

(e) Please explain the arrows on the DESIGN and BUSINESS sides.

_____

(f) The most difficult arrows to explain are the ones pointing to HISTORY. What does each of the side panels have to do with HISTORY?

Could a director benefit from reading about past productions of a play that he or she is producing?

Might a director improve his/her skills by reading the biography of another well-respected director?

Would knowledge of Elizabethan stages be useful to someone directing a Shakespearean play?

Should a director of *The Andersonville Trial* read a book about the prison at Andersonville, Georgia, during the Civil War?

Do directors ever provide program notes that explain why they decided to produce a particular play?

(g) Now, ask yourself again, "How do each of the side panels relate to HISTORY?" You may interpret "history" in any way you wish.

Now, ask yourself again, "How do each of the side panels relate to HISTORY?" You may interpret "history" in any way you wish.

> Quickly review Activities #6 through #10. You are expected to choose only *one* of these activities and complete it in class tomorrow.

ACTIVITY #6

Creating a Large Cube

Purpose of Activity #6

The student will create a larger version of the cube created in Activity #3. Students will decorate the sides of the cube with appropriate words and pictures illustrating the interconnective nature of theatre.

DIRECTIONS

1. Locate and cut up an old shoe box or a similar cardboard container. Create a second cube three or four times larger than the one you made for Activity #3.

2. Cover your cube with colored paper.

3. Locate an old play program which you can cut up. Cut out words and pictures or whole pages. Find ones which illustrate the different sides of the cube.

4. Tape your clippings onto an appropriate side of your cube. For example:

   (a) The title of the play and the author's name would go on top.

   (b) The cast list would go on Side #2 and so forth.

   (c) You may have the most difficulty finding items for the history side of the cube. Notes about past accomplishments of cast members and the production staff could be considered HISTORY.

Notes about past accomplishments of cast members and the production staff could be considered HISTORY.

ACTIVITY #7

Creating a Play Program

Purpose of Activity #7

The student will create a play program. Students will better understand the cooperative nature of theatre after creating a play program.

DIRECTIONS

1. Create an eight page program which would be appropriate for the next play production at your school.

2. Be sure all six sides of the Theatre Cube are represented in your program. Since the play may not yet be in rehearsal, you may create a fictional cast and crew.

3. Try to have part of a page devoted to each side of the cube. Advertising might be considered a part of BUSINESS.

4. It is not necessary to write about only one side of the cube on each page. For example, you may want to place the title of the play, author, director and cast on one sheet. That page can represent ACTING.

ACTIVITY #8

Creating a Mobile Model

Purpose of Activity #8

The student will create a mobile model. Students will better understand the collaborative nature of theatre after creating a mobile model.

Students will better understand the collaborative nature of theatre after creating a mobile model.

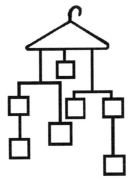

Activity #8 — Illustration 1

DIRECTIONS

1. Make a mobile using old wire hangers. Using string, scraps of cardboard and cut-out pictures, create the theatre cube concept in another manner.

2. Why do you think that Thomas Beagle chose a cube to represent theatre?

3. What does the shape and what do the arrows suggest about theatres and theatre people?

4. With your new mobile model, think of areas of theatre that were not emphasized on the simple cube model. Are there positions that the cube does not identify? Can you emphasize these areas visually in your mobile model?

5. Be prepared to display your mobile to classmates. Explain why you chose the shapes, pictures and relationships that you did.

ACTIVITY #9

Creating a Two-Dimensional Collage

Purpose of Activity #9

The student will create a two-dimensional collage representing his/her own vision of theatre. Students will better understand the collaborative nature of theatre after creating a two-dimensional collage.

A collage is a collection of photographs, news clippings, drawings, pieces of colorful materials, and found objects.

DIRECTIONS

1. Make a two-dimensional collage representing your vision of theatre. A collage is a collection of photographs, news clippings, drawings, pieces of colorful materials, and found objects.

2. Include all six categories of the cube in your collage.

3. These items should be arranged and glued into an artistic statement. Because of the arrangement, the viewer will understand what you feel is important about theatre.

4. Be prepared to display your collage to classmates. They will be asked to locate examples of different sides of the Theatre Cube in your collage.

ACTIVITY #10

Creating a Photographic Model

Purpose of Activity #10

The student will create a photographic model representing all six sides of the Theatre Cube. Students will better understand the collaborative nature of theatre after creating a photographic model.

DIRECTIONS

1. Photograph a current play production or cut out some pictures from a newspaper or magazine which describe the play.

2. Try to represent all six sides of the Theatre Cube with pictures.

3. Glue the photographs onto a box or display them on a poster.

Students will better understand the collaborative nature of theatre after creating a photographic model.

ACTIVITY #11

Questions That May Appear in an Oral Quiz

Your instructor has given you some class time to complete activities in this chapter. As part of your evaluation, you will be given an oral quiz. Your objective will be to show that you understand how a six-sided cube represents the concept of theatre.

Working in groups, students take turns asking and answering the following questions.

Purpose of Activity #11

To prepare for an oral quiz, students answer questions relating to the Theatre Cube.

DIRECTIONS

1. Students take turns reading aloud the following seven questions.

2. Students answer the questions as a team. They may wish to write down the answers to review later.

ORAL QUIZ QUESTIONS

1. What are the names of the six sides of a Theatre Cube model?

2. On which side of the cube would you place each of the following theatre jobs? Explain your choice.

Designer of the Program Cover	Playwright
Costume Designer	Assistant Director
Scene Painter	Pantomime Artist
Property Master	Box Office Manager
Wardrobe Mistress	Chorus Line Member
Play Program Copywriter	Stage Manager
Spotlight Operator	Usher

3. Choose one side of the cube. Can you explain the arrows drawn at each of the four borders of that panel?

4. Of what significance is the cube shape? Would a rectangular box be as good or a better form to represent the concept of theatre? Explain.

5. Explain how each of the following individuals in a play production might make use of the Theatre Cube model while rehearsing or getting ready for opening night.

   (a) Director, (b) Play Program Copywriter, (c) Publicity Chairperson, (d) Actor, (e) Host of the Party for Cast and Crew

6. Does HISTORY really deserve to be one of the six sides on the cube? Give reasons for your answer.

7. Do you find any problems with the placement of the six panels or the use of arrows on the Theatre Cube? If yes, do you have any suggestions to improve the model?

UNIT ONE SUMMARY

The Theatre Cube model reminds us that every person in a company performs an important function.

You have completed several projects in this short unit. Each activity was designed to illustrate the cooperative nature of theatre. You have been introduced to several new thoughts:

1. The Theatre Cube model reminds us that *every* person in a company performs an important function.

2. You need to understand the goals and ideas of others so that you can perform your own job competently.

3. In a theatre class or during a play rehearsal, you depend on every single person in the group to complete a job successfully.

4. Each person performing a role on-stage or behind the stage is connected to the entire team.

5. Everyone needs to work together cooperatively to achieve a successful performance.

EVALUATION GUIDELINES

In each unit in this course, you will be a member of a team. Your team will work collaboratively to make certain that everyone finishes his/her work and succeeds. The evaluation guidelines at the end of every unit will give maximum points to a student's contributions to the team.

Everyone needs to work together cooperatively to achieve a successful performance.

UNIT ONE EVALUATION GUIDELINES

Student completed Activity #3 with team on Day One.   (20)_____
    Cube neatly constructed.
    Sides labeled, arrows in place.

Completed second project on time.   (20)_____
    Imaginative.
    Carefully thought out and executed.

Can name the six sides of the Theatre Cube.   (10)_____

Arrived on time in class with appropriate materials.   (10)_____

Accepted offers of help from team members, worked hard,
and helped others on team.   (35)_____

Participated fully in group activities.   (20)_____

                                     Total _____

70-79 = C   80-89 = B   90-100 = A   101-115 = A+

NOTE

Theatre is a collaborative learning experience. The greatest number of points are given to students who work cooperatively with their group and who help others.

UNIT TWO
Introduction to Storytelling

Stories are entertaining to hear *and* to tell. The first ones we hear as children are usually told to us by a parent or grandparent. We come to know and love these tales before we are able to read or write. All the earliest stories of our civilization were passed down orally. These stories were told from generation to generation, long before the invention of writing.

Today, with television and movies, teenagers learn new stories by viewing them on a screen. Even myths and fairy tales are retold in Saturday morning cartoons. Yet we never lose that magical sense of wonder when somebody we admire takes the time to tell us a story.

Hearing a story without pictures allows us to use our imagination. A storyteller shares a feeling of warmth that a video or movie screen cannot duplicate. Storytelling is one of the earliest forms of "theatre." Actors can learn a great deal by practicing this ancient tradition.

Hearing a story without pictures allows us to use our imagination.

This unit on storytelling will give you experience in using your voice effectively. It will help you organize details for memorization, and use movement and gestures to reinforce meaning. At the same time you will be providing pleasure to a young audience of "admirers."

ACTIVITY #1

How Do You Become a Storyteller?
You Begin by Remembering...

Purpose of Activity #1

Students will learn the early steps a storyteller takes before selecting a tale to tell.

DIRECTIONS

1. Read paragraphs A, B, C, D, E and F.

2. Discuss any storytelling you may have performed in grade school or church, or any fears or concerns you may have about storytelling.

A. How do you begin telling stories? You begin by remembering those earliest experiences you had as a listener. Maybe you recall listening to your grandmother. Or a librarian. Or a teacher. Or an older brother or sister. You begin by remembering the stories that you enjoyed hearing. Try to remember why you liked a particular story. Did the teller "act out" the different voices in the story? Did the person move his or her body? Did the person look at you while he/she was telling the story?

B. Ask yourself some questions: 1. What stories do I know and love? 2. Who will be my listeners? What will their age group be? 3. What is the occasion for the storytelling? Is it a holiday or birthday party? 4. Is it a storytelling festival or a church function? 5. Will I be the only storyteller performing for the group? 6. How long should my story be?

C. Your teacher may help choose an audience for your storytelling. For example, your audience may be children six to nine years old. You can suggest specific groups that you think would appreciate a visit from some storytellers: an elementary school class, a Brownie or Cub Scout troop, a group of children at your church, or a children's hospital. Then you or your instructor can call the group to arrange a storytelling session.

Your group objective will be to entertain the children. Your personal objective will be to gain confidence and experience as a performer.

D. Your teacher will also help you select a story. Several stories, including folktales, a fable, and a myth are printed in the Appendix of this book. All are brief and appropriate for young audiences. Several students will be telling stories to the same group of listeners, so your tales must be short — five to seven minutes in length. Your *group objective* will be to entertain the children. Your *personal objective* will be to gain confidence and experience as a performer.

E. How do you gain confidence? You gain confidence from knowing that you are giving pleasure to other people. You are going to share a wonderful gift with your audience: yourself. Storytelling is magical. You must truly believe that oral tales of fact or fantasy actually have magical powers. You also must believe that ordinary people can tell these tales.

F. Listen carefully during this unit. Some early exercises will be aimed at rekindling your love of stories and developing your confidence. Listening, observing and practicing will prove to you that you have the ability to succeed as a storyteller.

ACTIVITY #2

Choosing Your Audience

Purpose of Activity #2

Students and their teacher will choose an audience for their storytelling performance.

DIRECTIONS

1. If you know who your audience will be, you will be better able to choose an appropriate story.

2. Each of the tales printed in the Appendix of this text is an appropriate story for young people, older adults, parents, or church groups.

3. Offer suggestions for possible audiences to your teacher.

4. Write the name of a potential audience on the form that follows or on the form that your instructor provides.

If you know who your audience will be, you will be better able to choose an appropriate story.

What is the name of the group for whom you would like to perform (for example: the Maryland School second grade class)?

_____

Age of audience: _____

What interests does this group have? _____

_____

ACTIVITY #3

Choosing a Story to Tell

Purpose of Activity #3

Each student will choose a tale to tell.

DIRECTIONS

1. Finding a tale you really like is the most important step to take in storytelling. Select a favorite story of your own. Or choose one of the stories provided by your teacher.

2. The age of your audience will be six- to nine-year-old children or older adults. Both young children and older adults enjoy similar stories, tales and fables. Your story should be five to seven minutes long.

3. Most tales are brief. Do not choose a tale just because it is a few sentences shorter than the others. Select the one that appeals to you the most. To tell a story convincingly, you have to like it. In fact, to tell it with enthusiasm, you have to love it.

4. Write the name of your selection on the form that follows or on the form that your instructor provides.

To tell a story convincingly, you have to like it. In fact, to tell it with enthusiasm, you have to love it.

Selection: _____

I think that children or older adults will like this story because

_____

_____

_____

I like this story because _____

_____

ACTIVITY #4

Understanding Your Story

Purpose of Activity #4

Students analyze and understand their tales by reading them aloud with a partner and discussing the tales.

DIRECTIONS

1. Working in pairs, students read aloud their tales to their partners.

2. After both students have read their tales out loud, they should take turns reading and listening to each other's story several times.

3. Read and discuss "How to Analyze and Understand Your Tale."

4. Complete the form, "Understanding Your Story."

HOW TO ANALYZE AND UNDERSTAND YOUR TALE

Discuss each of these questions and suggestions with your partner.

A. As you repeat your story, notice how details in the tale are repeated. (a) What is the first major problem or event? (b) What is the second major incident that changes the main character's life? (c) How many key events are there in all? (d) What is the last main event in the story? (e) Does the story end there? (f) If not, what is the purpose of the conclusion that follows?

B. Consider the opening of the story. (a) Does the listener need any background information about the main characters? (b) Does the story state *where* and *when* the events take place? (c) Do any details suggest the time of day or the mood of the story?

Does the story state **where** *and* **when** *the events take place?*

C. Are there any key objects in the story? A magic horn? A stolen box? A glass slipper? If so, describe the object to your partner. You should describe this item in greater detail than the printed tale describes it. Ask your partner to describe the same object. Repeat this exercise with an object from your partner's tale. This short exercise will get you started in stretching your imagination.

Identify the main parts of your story on the "Understanding Your Story" form on page 22, or on a form that your instructor provides.

UNDERSTANDING YOUR STORY

Title of story: _____

Characters:

_____   _____

_____   _____

Key object(s) in story: _____

_____

Other background information: _____

_____

_____

_____

_____

The first major event that occurs is: _____

_____

_____

The next key event: _____

_____

_____

The next major event or problem: _____

_____

_____

And the next: _____

_____

_____

The climax occurs when: _____

_____

_____

Conclusion: _____

_____

_____

ACTIVITY #5

It's Time to Practice Telling Your Story

Purpose of Activity #5

Students practice telling their tales to their partners and to other members of their smaller groups.

DIRECTIONS

1. Apply the "Five Practice Steps" in order to successfully tell your tale.

2. Practice telling your tale to a partner and to other members of your smaller group.

3. Read your story to yourself several times. Next, have your partner read the story out loud to you. It is important that you hear the words to your story as well as see them in print.

4. Your partner will read her tale silently. Then you will read your partner's tale to her so that she can hear the words of her story.

It is important that you hear the words to your story as well as see them in print.

FIVE PRACTICE STEPS

1. Each time you tell the story, check the written text. See if you have left out any important facts. You may decide that you need to memorize special words or sentences.

2. Put the story and your outline aside. Try to tell the tale in your own words. You can look at the outline if you wish. But you should no longer refer to the written version of the tale. Begin to use your own words as you tell the story. You can introduce phrases from the original tale, but it is important to add details of your own. Your goal is to entertain your audience.

3. Feel free to exaggerate your face and body movements. Larger hand, body and facial movements will appear natural to your listeners. These behaviors help capture the attention of the audience. They also help to create the characters you are portraying. Practice changing your voice. Make it low. Make it high. Make it mean. Your listeners will love it.

4. You want to be a success when you finally tell your story to a "live" audience. Therefore, make your interpretation of the

story unique. You are unique. Your story reflects you just as a mirror does. Look upon your story as a gift that you have decorated with your mind. You are sharing this gift with your listeners. Make the telling of the story a reflection of your personality as well as that of the original author.

5. Retell the story enough times so that you do not need notes or an outline. It is important that you know the basic details of your story well, for then you will be able to speak from memory. Your story will move smoothly. You will not have to stop and think of what to say next. Your audience will enjoy the story more if it moves quickly and easily.

ACTIVITY #6

More Tips and Practice

Purpose of Activity #6

Students practice the "Ten Storytelling Tips to Remember" in order to become successful storytellers.

DIRECTIONS

1. Students work in pairs.

2. Memorize the details in your story. Ask yourself how you can make the telling of the story more lively and interesting. Consider ways to develop your characters, strengthen key moments with appropriate actions and adjust the speed and volume of your voice.

3. Reveal the following information through your voice and actions. (a) Communicate the age of the people talking through the tone of your voice. (b) Reveal to your listeners whether the characters are mean or kind. (c) Reveal whether the people are rich or poor.

4. If you are portraying two characters in conversation, make a slight movement of your head to the left to show that one person is speaking. Next, make a movement to the right to show that the other person is now talking. Be careful, however. Extreme movements, such as abruptly turning your whole body, are awkward and not as effective.

5. Suggest personality changes with your voice and posture. Your goal is to encourage your listeners to use their imaginations. You want them to "see" these characters in their minds.

6. Use each of the following "Ten Storytelling Tips to Remember" as you practice your tale.

Suggest personality changes with your voice and posture. Your goal is to encourage your listeners to use their imaginations.

TEN STORYTELLING TIPS TO REMEMBER

1. **Develop separate behaviors for each character.** These behaviors will help both you and your listeners focus on which character is actually speaking. Focus on the following exaggerated movements:

   (a) If you roll your eyes, open them wide. Then roll them slowly.

   (b) Your character might stroke his chin before speaking. Stroke your chin slowly, with big hand movements up and down.

   (c) An old witch might hobble on a cane. Make her hobble slowly back and forth.

   Remember: you are an entertainer. Your audience expects your characters and their actions to be exaggerated.

2. **Choose a voice for each character.** A high pitch often suggests an animal, child, or female voice. If the animal is a bear or a big bad wolf, the pitch should be lower than normal. Low pitch also suggests that a male character is speaking. Change the speed in which you talk. Now you can express nervousness, sleepiness, or slyness. Try to develop a distinctly different voice for each character.

3. **Remember that you, the storyteller/narrator, are a character, too.** You should have a narrator voice that is distinct from the characters who talk.

4. **Develop a gesture that signals when you are switching from character to narrator.** Open your palms wide and bend your wrists and elbows back. It is a gesture that might accompany the line "Oh! What a surprise!" Then, whenever you open your palms wide, you are telling your audience: "Now I am the narrator." The open palm is traditionally a sign of "welcome" and "peace." It is less threatening than if you point your finger at audience members.

   Once your palms are extended, move your hands in a sideward movement. These hand gestures will keep the listener's attention focused on you. They enable the audience to follow the story more easily because they know when the narrator is talking. At first this technique may seem a little artificial, but it has proven successful for beginning storytellers.

5. **Look for descriptive details in the story or changes in the mood that you could reinforce with gestures, movement**

Remember: you are an entertainer. Your audience expects your characters and their actions to be exaggerated.

or vocal inflection. For example, at a moment of suspense, lower your voice. Slow down your delivery, pause and look sneaky, moving from left to right. This might also be a good time to get up from your seat. Move closer to your listeners so they can hear your whispers and feel your tension.

6. **Remember, good eye contact with audience members builds a bond between teller and listener.** The eye contact should not be limited to the times when you are the "narrator." When characters in the story talk, they should look at individual members of the audience. Looking at people right in the eye makes them a part of the story. This practice makes storytelling different from a "regular play." The storyteller involves the listeners. The audience imagines the settings. They "see" the characters in their minds. Help your listeners visualize how characters are dressed and whether they are scared, tempted or sad.

Eye contact is the best way to get listeners to become involved in the storytelling process.

Eye contact is the best way to get listeners to become involved in the storytelling process. You are helping them learn to use their imaginations. As you practice you will not have an audience of children. However, you must imagine that you have an audience before you. Pretend to make eye contact with the "spaces" that will someday be occupied by "listeners."

7. **Use eye movements to pretend to "see" objects and other characters in the story.** Make these objects or people seem real to yourself. Support these imaginary props or people by shaping or reaching toward them with hand gestures. Try looking away occasionally to reestablish eye contact with audience members. Try to use hand movements for emphasis in many parts of your tale. Hand movements help focus listener attention on you and your story.

8. **For a beginning storyteller, movement is essential.** Move around a lot. If you have a large audience, be sure you walk over to the people at the extreme edges. Move from far left to far right and back again. Movement will help you to make eye contact with all of your listeners. Moreover, when you are moving, you are sending messages of energy to your audience. These are unspoken messages. They say, "I am involved. Won't you become involved with me?" Trained by television, today's young audiences expect movement. Watch "Sesame Street" or MTV. Note how many times in a minute the images on the screen change.

Some excellent storytellers remain seated on purpose. They create energy by leaning out toward their listeners. They use hand gestures and make excellent eye contact.

However, for this unit, you are going to stay on your feet. You are going to incorporate lots of movement in your telling. You may use a chair as a prop and occasionally sit down. But you are going to be up and out of that seat and moving most of the time. Choose five or six places in your tale where movement and gestures will strengthen the meaning. Mark those places on your copy of the story. Indicate where and how you will move.

9. **After you have made these notations, retell your story several more times.** Concentrate on developing your character and adding movement. At first you may want to practice in private with a tape recorder. However, after a day of working alone, have a classmate observe your storytelling. Your partner can then provide you with suggestions about your voice, movements and gestures. Remember to mark places where you need to change your voice to suit each character.

10. **In return, one of your responsibilities will be to become a listener and responder to your partner.** If you observe well, you may pick up some new techniques. You might adapt and use some of your partner's methods in your own presentation. Ask your partner if she minds if you adapt her movements, gestures, or "voices."

Naturally, you will want to maintain your own individuality as storyteller. But you will not be a copycat if you borrow a subtle gesture, an effective pause, or an appropriate descriptive word. Many great storytellers imitate gestures and movements that they have observed in other storytellers.

Many great storytellers imitate gestures and movements that they have observed in other storytellers.

Be sure to praise your partner when providing feedback. All storytellers need to hear what they are doing well. You also need to point out which parts of their telling could be improved. Be kind when you point out weaknesses. Try to suggest specific ways that problem areas may be improved. When two storytellers listen to one another in practice, their goal should be *to help* and *to learn*.

ACTIVITY #7

Fixing the Rough Spots

Purpose of Activity #7

Each student will apply the following three suggestions and the "Nine Techniques to Fix the Rough Spots" in order to tell his/her tale more competently and successfully.

DIRECTIONS

1. Students work in pairs. Practice telling your tale to your partner and to other members of your group.

2. **Suggestion #1**: Isolate one, two, or three sections of your story. Repeat just those parts. Try to find the most appropriate way to phrase or emphasize the necessary facts.

3. **Suggestion #2**: Close your eyes. See the characters, the surroundings or the action in your mind.

4. **Suggestion #3**: Describe in detail what you see in your mind.

5. Apply the following "Nine Techniques to Fix the Rough Spots" in order to perform your tale more successfully.

You know your strengths and you know the areas in which you need improvement. Now you need to practice a smooth delivery.

In Activities #5 and #6, your instructor and partner may have told you some things about your storytelling. You know your strengths and you know the areas in which you need improvement. Now you need to practice a smooth delivery.

This is hard work. You need to be inventive and persistent. Be as specific as you can. Plan gestures, movements and eye contact. After the repetitions and experimentation, find other sections of the tale of which you are uncertain. Ask your partner to help you work on these rough spots. Use the following techniques as you practice your telling.

NINE TECHNIQUES TO FIX THE ROUGH SPOTS

1. Close your eyes and try to visualize that difficult segment of the story as a silent movie. How would the actors in that movie express their feelings without the use of words? What

gestures would they use? What props? Would the camera zoom in for any close-ups?

2. Run the scene through your mind several times. Then run it backward. What are the essential parts of that scene? Next, open your eyes. Keep the scene playing in your mind. Describe the scene. Now become the characters in it.

3. Create a new character: a servant, a pet, or a spider on the wall. Introduce that new character. Describe the events in the difficult segment of the story from that character's point of view. This fresh point of view may produce new excitement in the story. It may also help you get past a difficult section of the story.

> **Example:** "Outside the ballroom a servant saw a scullery maid. She was running down a hallway. Then she disappeared through a side door. Moments later the Prince, himself, appeared and asked the servant,
>
> 'Did you see a beautiful princess come from the ballroom?'
>
> 'No, Your Majesty, but a ragged maid just went down that hallway.'
>
> 'Well, find her and ask her if she saw a princess.'
>
> Then the servant dashed down the hall and out the door, but he found no one. Glancing down, he spied a little glass slipper."

4. Often, the very beginning of the story poses a problem. Possibly, "Once upon a time..." seems boring. Alternative phrases sound clumsy or awkward. At this point, forget the beginning and the end of the story. For now, master movement and character development. You can work on the beginning later.

5. Try to retell the rest of the tale perfectly. Pay attention to the high point of the story — the climax. Remember to punctuate important words with actions and emotions. Get details in the right order. Details add force to your sentences. All of these activities require several practice sessions.

6. If you are working with a partner, tell the difficult segment of the story to your partner. Tell it a second time. Then have your partner tell it back to you. Possibly he or she will leave

Describe the events in the difficult segment of the story from that character's point of view. This fresh point of view may produce new excitement in the story.

out one or two details or change a description. Ask yourself, "Would some of those changes help me?"

7. Sometimes a storyteller feels too tied to the printed story. Remember: You can make little changes or add an explanation the original story did not provide. These changes allow the storyteller to visualize the tale more clearly. They also help the storyteller to feel a stronger ownership of the tale.

8. Do not forget the rest of the story. You should separate and repeat those sections that you feel need the most work. However, you must also keep practicing the parts that are working well.

9. Tell the full story from beginning to end. You will feel more confident about certain parts that have proven troublesome.

A good storyteller does more than present the facts. You must grasp your listeners' attention.

By now you know the facts in your story. But do not relax yet. A good storyteller does more than present the facts. You must grasp your listeners' attention. You must convince them that your story is a tale they will remember.

ACTIVITY #8

Introductions and Conclusions

Purpose of Activity #8

Students learn to begin and end their tales in a relaxed, experienced manner.

DIRECTIONS

1. You will work in pairs as you practice your tales in Activity #8.

2. Practice telling your tale first to your partner and then to other members of your group.

3. Apply the following "Eight Suggestions for Introducing and Concluding Your Story" to your tale.

EIGHT SUGGESTIONS FOR INTRODUCING AND CONCLUDING YOUR STORY

How do you capture your listeners' attention right from the start? You plan and practice your introduction with great care. You are now ready to practice the beginning of your tale. "Once upon a time..." and an indication of the setting and main characters should be fine. Keep your energy level high. This is not the time to feel shy. As a storyteller you need to be noticed and listened to. You also want to make all members of your audience feel as if you are talking to them individually.

1. Eye contact is the best tool you have to secure your listeners' attention. You may begin your presentation in silence. Quietly observe the members of the audience. Really "see" them. Cover the entire group from left to right and then from front to back. Then look from right to left and from back to front.

   Eye contact is the best tool you have to secure your listeners' attention.

2. You may choose to begin by talking to the audience. Move across the performance area from one side of the audience to the other. Then move back again. Make eye contact with as many individuals as you can. The way you pronounce the opening words of your tale and the way you look at the audience tells them something. You make it clear that you have a story that they are going to enjoy.

3. Should you announce the title of the story and give any background about its origin? Should you tell your audience who you are? Probably. Some requirements may be set by your teacher.

   Remember: As soon as you move into the area in front of the audience, you are "on-stage." How you say your name and announce the title will influence how well your story is received.

4. When you open the actual story, make it short. Do not bother with lengthy descriptions of characters or places. Instead, move quickly to the action. Action captures everyone's attention. If you have trouble telling the beginning of the story the same way twice, write the first two sentences. Then memorize them! Write short sentences. They should establish time, place, and character: *When, Where* and *Who*.

5. The end of a tale is easier to tell. Plan and practice your conclusion with almost as much care as you do the introduction. You want your audience to remember and cherish you and your tale.

6. Does your story have a moral? If so, what is it? Are you sure? Sometimes after working with a story, a storyteller realizes

that the tale has a deeper meaning than he or she originally thought. If a story does have a moral, do you want to state it? Or do you want to leave it unstated so that the audience can talk about it afterward?

7. Like the introduction, the conclusion should be fairly short. It can summarize: what happened to the main characters, or to the village they lived in, or to an object that figured prominently in the plot. The ending might hint at a moral by having one of the characters speak at the end. A character may comment about how he or she will behave in the future. As a narrator, you could point to some modern day customs that suggest that human nature does *not* really change over the years.

8. You want to end confidently. Therefore, write and memorize the final two sentences that you will speak. Then practice saying those two sentences. Decide on a set of gestures that will give emphasis to the most important words. Last, decide which gestures will indicate clearly that your story is over.

After working on the introduction and conclusion, practice the complete tale several times from beginning to end. You are now ready for an audience.

> ***Enthusiasm and a desire to share a good tale will win your audience's respect and approval.***

You may not feel that you are ready to tell your story. All actors feel that they are never ready. If you believe in your story, you do not have to be perfect in your telling. Enthusiasm and a desire to share a good tale will win your audience's respect and approval. Most listeners will not even notice slight mistakes and changes. Your audience will love you. And they will love your story.

ACTIVITY #9

Performing Before an Audience

All the activities trained you for this final performance. The analyzing, the planning and the practice are not important unless you have a live audience with whom to share your story. Fellow classmates provided your first audience. They provided someone with whom to make eye contact and someone to share your tale.

Your teacher may have scheduled your storytelling session with a class of elementary students. If students have prepared the same stories, your teacher will arrange for them to perform before different classes in one school.

After you have completed your performance, you may want to entertain other groups. A group at your church may enjoy listening to your tale. Storytelling is enjoyable not only for the listener, but for the teller as well.

Storytelling is enjoyable not only for the listener, but for the teller as well.

Purpose of Activity #9

Students fulfill the goal of Unit Two by performing their tales before an audience.

DIRECTIONS

1. Each student will perform a storytelling for a kindergarten class, a first or second grade class, or an older adult group.

2. You may wish to perform a second storytelling for a group of Cub Scouts, Brownies, a reading at a library, a nursery school, or a birthday party for six-year-olds. In that case, more responsibility will be placed on *your* shoulders. However, you will be pleased by the joy and warmth of your young audiences.

3. As you tell your story, keep your energy high and have fun. Remember that your tale is a gift. Unfold it lovingly. Help your listeners see the bright colors with which you have wrapped your story. Let them discover the beautiful contents inside your tale. Finally, soak in the applause when you reach the end! Take a deep bow. You earned it!

UNIT TWO SUMMARY

This unit has introduced you to the art and pleasure of storytelling. In addition to bringing happiness and enjoyment to your audience, you have gained confidence and skill as a storyteller. This joyful art has been practiced for thousands of years. *You* are continuing the great tradition.

In Unit Two you have learned:

1. To select a tale which you enjoy that is appropriate for your listeners.

2. To analyze the structure of a story.

   a. To determine where and when the story takes place.

b. To search for the key events.

c. To understand the characters and their behaviors.

d. To look for important objects in the tale.

3. To organize details for memorization.

4. To use movement and gestures to reinforce the meaning of the tale.

5. To use eye contact to capture and retain audience attention.

6. To provide constructive criticism for a fellow student.

7. To observe and to listen to fellow storytellers and to learn from their examples.

8. To keep alive an age-old tradition.

> *This joyful art [storytelling] has been practiced for thousands of years. You **are** continuing the great tradition.*

UNIT TWO EVALUATION GUIDELINES

In each unit in this course, you will be a member of a team. That team will work collaboratively to make certain that everyone finishes his/her work and succeeds. The evaluation guidelines at the end of every unit will give maximum points to a student's contributions to the team.

MEETING DEADLINES

1. Participated fully in Activities #4, #5, #6, #7 and #8.   (20) _____

2. Memorized story by Day Seven and took pride in doing quality work.   (25) _____

3. Arrived on time ready to work with partner.   (10) _____

COLLABORATIVE TEAM EFFORT

4. Accepted offers of help from team members, worked hard and helped others on team.   (30) _____

5. Offered help to partner and provided cooperative support.   (30) _____

Total _____

70-79 = C   80-89 = B   90-100 = A   101-115 = A+

NOTE

Theatre is a collaborative learning experience. The greatest number of points are given to students who work cooperatively with their group and who help others.

EVALUATION GUIDELINES

Several units in this text end with some type of performance. A Performance Evaluation form follows. You may wish to use this checklist to evaluate your success as a storyteller. The same form will appear at the conclusion of other chapters.

Your instructor may have more than one set of criteria for arriving at a grade. However, if you honestly believe that you deserve a rating of 3 or 4 in each category of the following chart, you can probably be sure that your grade for this unit will be an A or a B.

Theatre Class Performance Evaluation

Name _____

Project _____

	EXCELLENT (4)	GOOD (3)	FAIR (2)	POOR (1)	NONE (0)
MEMORIZATION, PREPARATION					
MOVEMENT, BLOCKING					
CONCENTRATION					
ARTICULATION, DICTION					
PROJECTION					
EXPRESSION, CHARACTERIZATION					
RATE OF SPEECH					
POISE, STAGE PRESENCE, APPEARANCE					
ENERGY, CREATIVITY					
OVERALL EFFECT					
READY ON TIME					
Subtotals					
Total					

Introduction to Playwriting

Most students are involved in some kind of "theatre" from the time they are very young. Do you remember when you and your friends assumed the roles of people in a movie or soap opera? Or maybe you created your own "play." Then, in the backyard, everyone pretended to be the different characters in the play.

Some students participate in plays at school, scouts, or church. Maybe a teacher, student, or parent writes the play. Often students perform their plays in a classroom, the cafeteria, the middle of any room, or even outdoors. Actors do not need a formal stage to present a play.

Exactly what is "theatre"? One definition for theatre is: one or more actors acting out a story before an audience on a bare stage. However, most theatre projects also involve a written script or play.

Plays are written for actors to perform. Normally two or more characters are involved in a struggle. We call that struggle the dramatic plot. The following activities introduce you to the elements of dramatic plot. They encourage you to experience the playwright's craft.

Normally two or more characters are involved in a struggle. We call that struggle the dramatic plot.

The basic structure for writing a play was created long ago in Greece around 400 B.C. Today most new playwrights begin their careers by learning and applying this traditional structure for telling a dramatic story. Furthermore, as writers become experienced, most playwrights still choose to follow this pattern when they create new plays.

Unit Three is an introduction to playwriting. You may not actually write a complete play in Unit Three. However, each activity will give you the skills for writing other play scripts in the future. We guarantee that you will have an enjoyable experience in Unit Three.

ACTIVITY #1

Getting Started

The Playwriting Game: Storyboard teaches you basic playwriting terms. These special words are used to describe the traditional structure of dramatic plot. Remembering this playwriting vocabulary will aid you in developing a play that makes sense.

Stories that are logical and make sense are easier to write. After you have created your outline, you will be able to write a script more quickly. The words will flow more easily when you know *who* and *what* you are writing about.

Stories that are logical and make sense are easier to write.

Purpose of Activity #1

Each team will write the outline of a short story or play in thirty minutes.

Each team of students will participate in *The Playwriting Game: Storyboard*. Activity #1 enables students to outline a play the way professional writers create scripts.

THE PLAYWRITING GAME: STORYBOARD
How to Outline a Play in Thirty Minutes

DIRECTIONS

1. Play *Storyboard*, Game 1. You will play this game with four or five teammates. Playing this game with a small group gives you a chance to tell other people what you think and feel. It also gives your team members an opportunity to express their opinions.

2. Your team will use several items that your teacher gives you to play this game: (a) the directions, (b) a game-board, (c) eight different sets of game cards, (d) Post-it™ notes to stick onto your game cards, (e) and a *Storyboard* Summary Sheet for each team member. Players work as a team when choosing the first five cards. Team members take turns selecting or suggesting incidents.

   NOTE: The rules stress that players make an effort to agree on all their choices.

3. You will quickly understand the game board. Fourteen numbered squares form a path on which you will place cards. Some cards will describe the characters in your play. Other cards will describe a series of events. These incidents occur in chronological order. That means that one event may occur on Thursday night, the next on Friday afternoon, and the third incident on Saturday morning.

4. Visualize the details of the story. Put yourself in a character's place. Imagine how you would talk or feel. Imagine what the setting looks like. When none of the cards quite meets your needs, use a Post-it™ note to express your thoughts. You may also use a Post-it™ note to add extra details to a card.

5. Try changing the order in which your team places cards on the board. You may wish to shift cards forward a space or backward two spaces. Moving cards around to different numbered squares may improve the logic and flow of your story. However, please note: the Resolution Card always comes *at the end* of your story.

6. TEAM OBJECTIVE: Work together to develop an interesting dramatic plot. Remember: When your team finishes the game, copy the necessary information from each square of your storyboard onto a *Storyboard* Summary Sheet. Later, you will want to rewrite these outlines into lines of dialog and dramatic scenes.

7. Remember to complete the Summary Sheet. Once you take the cards off the game board, it is difficult to recall the story accurately.

8. If time permits, you may wish to play *Storyboard* a second time. Afterward, share your team's stories with other groups.

> *Work together to develop an interesting dramatic plot.*

ACTIVITY #2

Learning the Vocabulary of a Playwright

Purpose of Activity #2

Each class member will learn the vocabulary that a playwright uses.

```
DIRECTIONS
```

1. Read aloud the "Glossary: Playwriting Vocabulary."

2. Discuss the meaning of each word. Many of these words are ones that most students have never heard before. Do not be embarrassed if you do not know them. Try to use some of these words when you next play *Storyboard*.

3. You will learn the meaning of these words once you complete game two of *The Playwriting Game: Storyboard*.

GLOSSARY: PLAYWRITING VOCABULARY

The Playwriting Game: Storyboard uses six basic terms to describe the framework of a play script. This list also defines fifteen other terms which will be used later in reference to playwriting. This glossary is provided as an aid to help you to communicate more clearly with fellow playwrights.

SETTING: the place where the action in a play occurs. (*Storyboard* has *setting* cards.)

CHARACTERS: the people in a play. (*Storyboard* has *character* cards.)

PROTAGONIST: the main character who wants to change things for the better.

ANTAGONIST: the character, group, law, or obstacle in nature that stands in the way of the protagonist and the change he or she wishes to make.

Conflict...a battle between the desires of a protagonist and the obstacles created by the antagonist.

FOIL: a character whose main purpose is to aid the author in revealing facts about or the thoughts of another character.

INCIDENTS: things that happen in a play. (*Storyboard* has *incident* cards.)

CONFLICT: a battle between the desires of a protagonist and the obstacles created by the antagonist. (*Storyboard* has *conflict* cards.)

CRISIS: a point near the end of a dramatic plot when something must happen to bring the conflict to a "boil"; often synonymous with the climax. (*Storyboard* has *crisis* cards.)

CLIMAX: the point of highest excitement or tension in the story; a turning point in the protagonist's struggle to overcome an obstacle; see *crisis*.

RESOLUTION: the end of the story; the final details of the dramatic plot which reveal how the conflict came out. (*Storyboard* has *resolution* cards.)

DRAMATIC ACTION: any movement on-stage, any gesture or facial expression, and any tonal inflection that helps define a character's feelings or the conflict between two characters.

DIALOG: a sequence of spoken lines written for two or more actors to perform.

MONOLOG: a long speech spoken by a single character on-stage; other characters may be present.

STAGE DIRECTIONS: instructions added to the dialog of a written script to suggest movement, feelings, or tone of voice; they may also identify off-stage noises, describe a setting or character, or provide background information. Stage directions are either written in italics or enclosed in parentheses.

PLAY: a story that is told mostly with dialog and with some stage directions. Authors write plays with the hope that they will be performed by actors before an audience rather than read like a novel or short story.

ACT: a major division in a play. Modern day, full-length plays are usually divided into two or three acts, and audiences take an intermission between acts. Shorter plays are often called one-act plays.

SCENE: a smaller division of a play; part of an act which shows characters reacting to an important incident in the story.

FRENCH SCENE: a scene within a play in which the number of characters on the stage remains constant; it may be extremely short (the entrance and exit of a messenger) or it could last a whole act.

FLASHBACK: a storytelling device, first used in motion pictures, in which time and/or place changes abruptly. The audience sees what is happening somewhere else, side by side with the present. Or the audience gets a peek at a past event that influenced the behavior of one or more of the characters in the present scene.

A STAGED READING: an experimental reading of a script which is not intended to be a polished production. Actors move around to suggest spatial relationships on-stage. They use their voices to suggest tone and emotional feelings. Actors

Monolog: a long speech spoken by a single character on-stage...

may use a few chairs and a table but will often just pantomime other props.

A STORYBOARD: a diagram model of a series of events in a scene, a play, or a TV commercial. Storyboards use a row of panels like a comic strip. The story may be told with words or pictures or a combination of words and pictures.

ACTIVITY #3

Reading Lines of Dialog

A "dialog" is a sequence of spoken lines written for two or more characters in a scene. Activity #4 will ask you to write twenty lines of dialog. However, first you are going to read dialog. Following is a scene between two people named Harry and Louise. The first scene was written without stage directions. The second scene included stage directions for the actors to read. Read both scenes out loud. What do you like best about the dialog?

Purpose of Activity #3

After reading aloud the spoken lines for "Harry & Louise," Take 1, two characters in a short scene, students will better understand how to write simple, everyday conversations for a play.

After reading aloud the spoken lines for "Harry & Louise"... students will better understand how to write simple, everyday conversations for a play.

DIRECTIONS

1. Two students read aloud the parts of "Harry & Louise," Take 1. This first scene has no stage directions.

2. Answer the following questions after reading Take 1. (a) Why is Harry on the telephone? (b) Is Louise in the room when the scene begins? (c) Are there any other questions about this scene that the writer has not explained clearly?

3. Two students now read aloud the parts of "Harry & Louise," Take 2. This scene has been rewritten. The writer now has included stage directions.

4. Answer the following questions after seeing Take 2. (a) What are stage directions? (b) Why do writers use stage directions? (c) Would you include any stage directions for this scene that the writer overlooked? If so, what stage directions would you add to this scene?

HARRY & LOUISE: TAKE 1

HARRY: Operator? I seem to have been cut off. I was calling, long distance, to Toronto, Canada. Can you help me? The number I was calling was…

LOUISE: Well, the back door is bolted, and I unplugged the toaster.

HARRY: What are you doing with that knife?!

LOUISE: Oh, my goodness. I just cut a piece of…

HARRY: No, operator, I wasn't talking to you. My wife just… Look, operator, I'll call back in a moment.

LOUISE: …string to tie the tag onto our luggage, and I…

HARRY: Boy! You gave me a fright there for a moment.

Note that the above dialog is somewhat difficult to follow. It seems to begin the dramatic action in the middle of things. The reader may wonder, "Why is Harry on the phone?" and "Is Louise in the room when the scene starts?"

The writer could clarify these readers' questions by adding a few stage directions. If you decide to use stage directions in Activity #4 when you write your own twenty lines of dialog, keep stage directions brief and enclose all stage directions in parentheses. Place them in the script where they best seem to fit.

If you decide to use stage directions when you write your own twenty lines of dialog, keep [them] brief…

Using Stage Directions When You Write Dialog

"Harry & Louise," Take 2 has been rewritten by the author to illustrate how stage directions can enhance dialog. Find three ways in which the writer made this scene more understandable to you, the reader, and to the actors by adding stage directions.

HARRY & LOUISE: TAKE 2

(The scene is a living room. HARRY, alone On-stage, sits at a desk with a telephone receiver to his ear. He is trying to reach the hotel where he and LOUISE will be staying.)

HARRY: Operator? I seem to have been cut off. I was calling, long distance, to Toronto, Canada. Can you help me? The number I was calling was… *(LOUISE enters from the kitchen with a knife clutched in her right hand.)*

LOUISE: Well, the back door is bolted, and I unplugged the toaster.

HARRY: *(Seeing LOUISE)* What are you doing with that knife?!

LOUISE: Oh, my goodness. I just cut a piece of...

HARRY: *(Into phone)* No, operator, I wasn't talking to you. My wife just... Look, operator, I'll call back in a moment. *(Hangs up phone.)*

LOUISE: ...string to tie the tag onto our luggage, and I...

HARRY: Boy! You gave me a fright there for a moment.

Stage directions are discussed in more detail in a later activity.

ACTIVITY #4

Writing Twenty Lines of Dialog

Purpose of Activity #4

You will gain experience writing twenty lines of dialog for one scene from the play that your team outlined.

DIRECTIONS

1. Select two characters from the play that your team outlined on Day One. Use the same setting card.

2. Read the following section titled, "Learning to Write a Scene: Two Easy Steps." Then write twenty lines of dialog for the characters in *your* scene.

3. Review your twenty lines of dialog with team members after you have written them. Check to see if you used some of the elements for dramatic plot in your script:

   - Characters
   - Setting
   - Incidents
   - Conflict
   - Crisis
   - Resolution

4. Reread your dialog. Does your scene have a mini-crisis? The structure of a short scene often mirrors the structure of an entire play. The scene may be missing a resolution. However, it usually builds toward some sort of mini-crisis. This tension buildup makes your viewer or reader want to find out what happens next. Add additional lines so that the scene ends with a crisis.

The structure of a short scene often mirrors the structure of an entire play.

LEARNING TO WRITE A SCENE:
TWO EASY STEPS

Step 1. Think of this scene as an episode in a television soap opera. Write the lines of dialog as you imagine the characters in your soap opera or story might actually say them. Try to capture in writing the way people actually talk and think in "real life."

Try to capture in writing the way people actually talk and think in "real life."

Step 2. Each team member chooses a separate incident within the plot. Then that team member writes a scene about the incident. After each person writes his/her scene, your team will have completed four or five individual brief scenes for a play. Later your team may be able to combine all of these scenes into one play.

For this exercise, assume that two characters are in conflict.

Name for Character A (protagonist) _____

Name for Character B (antagonist) _____

Character A wants to _____

but Character B is an obstacle to that desire in that he/she ___

_____

ACTIVITY #5

Writers' Response Groups

Professional writers, including playwrights, often read their unfinished work to other professional writers. Students in creative writing classes do the same thing. The purpose of writers' response groups is to provide guidance, understanding, help and honest feedback about work in progress.

Writers gather in response groups to find out which lines of dialog communicate well. They also will debate which lines of dialog should be eliminated or rewritten. Your team will participate as members of a writers' response group while you are working on Activities #5, #6, #7 and #9 in this unit.

Purpose of Activity #5

Each student will understand the purpose of a writers' response group and will learn how to participate in a writers' response group.

```
 ┌─────────────────┐
 │ DIRECTIONS      │
 └─────────────────┘
```

1. Read the section titled, "Guidelines for Working in a Writers' Response Group" that follows.

2. Discuss points B, C, D and E.

3. Read the section titled, "Ten Questions Writers Ask in a Response Group."

Guidelines for Working in a Writers' Response Group

How a Writers' Response Group Works

A. Author A reads aloud the script he/she has written. At Author A's request, one or more other members of the group do a "cold" reading of the dialog. A "cold" reading means that the readers have never seen the words before. They can be expected to stumble over some words and mispronounce others.

B. After the reading, all members of the group take turns to briefly tell Author A what they liked *best* about the scene.

C. These same responders take turns again in expressing additional feelings about the scene. This time they may offer constructive criticism.

D. Author A has a chance to ask the group specific questions regarding what they have said, or what they have left unsaid. Samples of questions an author might ask are listed on page 47.

E. The group follows the same procedure using Author B's script, then Author C's script, etc.

Writers gather in response groups to learn which lines of dialog work well and conversely, to learn which sections or lines need more work.

Writers gather in response groups to learn which lines of dialog work well and, conversely, to learn which sections or lines need more work.

Ten Questions Writers Ask in a Response Group

In seeking answers to what works well in the dialog you have written, and which sections or lines need more work, you may wish to ask team members to answer some of the following questions:

1. Do you understand the *central conflict* in this scene that I wrote? Yes ❑   No ❑

   Can you put it into words? Yes ❑   No ❑

   If yes, then please do.

2. Which lines in this script first make you aware of the conflict? Please explain.

3. Does the scene I wrote make you want to know what happens next? Yes ❑   No ❑

   What do you think will happen following this scene? Please explain to the group.

4. Are my characters believable? Yes ❑   No ❑

   Does the dialog I have written sound like real people talking? Yes ❑   No ❑

   What personality traits are implied? To see if I was successful, please explain to the group which traits you thought were implied.

5. When character _____ says _____, do you understand what is happening? Yes ❑   No ❑

   Do I need to provide more stage directions?
   Yes ❑   No ❑

6. Do you understand why character _____ says _____?
   Yes ❑   No ❑

7. Is the scene long enough? Or is it too long? Explain.

8. Overall, how would you describe this scene I wrote: Funny? Sad? Suspenseful? Bizarre? Violent? Other?

9. What can I add (or take out) to improve the scene? Have the group explain clearly and in detail.

10. Did you enjoy listening to the dialog? Which part did you enjoy the most? Why did you like that part best?

> *Does the scene I wrote make you want to know what happens next?*

ACTIVITY #6

Writing More Dialog

Purpose of Activity #6

You gain further experience writing lines of dialog for a scene from the play that your team outlined on Day One.

DIRECTIONS

1. Select two characters from the play that your team outlined on Day One. Use the same setting card.

2. You will develop a scene in which you use *one* of the following cards selected by your team on Day One: (a) *one* incident card, (b) the conflict card, or (c) the crisis card. Write twenty more lines of dialog between the two characters in this *new* scene.

3. Ask yourself questions. Are the characters friends? Did they used to be friends? Are the characters in love with one another? Did they used to be in love with one another? Are the characters related to one another? Is there a conflict between them? Does one character have a secret? Does another character have a special problem? Recall your neighbors, friends, or relatives. Characters and stories exist all around you.

4. Pretend that you are writing for a television soap opera. Pretending makes writing dialog easier. Good writing is a skill that takes practice. Learning to write dialog is no different than learning to skate, play football, or dance. You have to practice if you want to write well.

Learning to write dialog is no different than learning to skate, play football, or dance. You have to practice if you want to write well.

ACTIVITY #7

Creating a Third Short Scene

Purpose of Activity #7

Each student gains further experience writing lines of dialog for a third short scene using the characters, incidents, conflict, crisis and resolution chosen by their team when they played *The Playwriting Game: Storyboard* on Day One.

DIRECTIONS

1. Write a scene that is different from the other two that you have created. Write twenty more lines of dialog.

2. Do you need new ideas? Consider the following suggestions:

   A. Write a *new* scene involving one or both of the characters you wrote about in Activity #4. The new scene might be one that comes before the scene already written. Or it could involve a crisis that comes after your completed scene. You may wish to include another character from the ones your team chose on Day One. You will be able to quickly create conflicts and problems in your characters' lives.

   B. Again, ask yourself the same questions that you asked in Activity #6. Are the characters friends? Did they used to be friends? Are the characters in love with one another? Did they used to be in love with one another? Are the characters related to one another? Is there a conflict between them? Does one character have a secret? Does another character have a special problem? Think of your neighbors, friends, or relatives. Characters and stories exist all around you.

   C. Imagine that you are writing for a television soap opera. Write about everyday people, problems, and situations. Make your dialog sound like the conversations you hear in real life.

   D. Remember when you and your classmates were reading your scenes to one another? Did someone else's story interest you? Write a *sequel* to his/her scene. Create new conflicts and problems and friendships. At the top of your paper write the name of the classmate who provided the idea for this scene. Begin writing the new scene and include stage directions with your dialog.

Think of your neighbors, friends, or relatives. Characters and stories exist all around you.

ACTIVITY #8

Actions Speak Louder Than Words

Most likely you have already included some stage directions in your scenes. But did you consider all the ways movement can add interest and suspense to your script? Examine the following brief scene as an example.

Purpose of Activity #8

Students will read the "Sara and Ruth" scene, Take 1 and Take 2, and will understand how stage directions help the actor, reader and viewer better understand a scene.

DIRECTIONS

1. Two students read aloud the parts of "Sara and Ruth," Take 1.

2. Two other students read aloud the parts of "Sara and Ruth," Take 2.

3. Discuss the differences between the two scenes. Is Take 2 easier to understand? What changes have been made by the writer? Explain why you think Take 2 is clearer and more interesting than Take 1.

SARA AND RUTH: TAKE 1

(A living room. The phone rings as SARA enters from the kitchen.)

SARA: *(Picks up phone.)* **Hello. Oh, hi, Lisa! Yes, I got here before she did, but I still don't know how I'm going to break the news to Mom that I got a kitten from the Humane Society. I think she'll let me keep it, but she's not going to be happy I did this without asking ahead of time.** *(Pause)* **Well, I have the kitty in the basement right now. She's so cute!** *(Noise of car Off-stage)* **Oops! A car just drove up. I think it's my mother. I don't want to be here when she arrives. Gotta go. Bye.** *(Hangs up phone and dashes up the hallway stairs.)*

(Car door slams Off-stage. We hear a key turn in the latch and the door open. Moments later, RUTH enters and calls toward the kitchen.)

RUTH: **Sara! Hi, Sara. You making dinner?** *(No answer.*

RUTH moves to the stairs.) **Sara! You upstairs, honey?** *(Pause)*

SARA: *(Off-stage, upstairs)* **Hello.**

RUTH: **Thought you said you'd start dinner if you got home ahead of me. Boy, am I exhausted. I worked my tail off today.**

SARA: *(Runs down the stairs.)* **I just got home myself. I'll go start dinner.** *(She heads for the kitchen.)*

RUTH: **Did you study at Lisa's house for your science test? It must have taken a long time. You should have been home hours ago.**

SARA: *(Stops.)* **Well, we talked for a while, then we got bored. So Lisa and I went for a ride in Lisa's car.** *(Continues toward kitchen.)*

RUTH: **Where did you go?** *(SARA stops.)* **Did you two go shopping?**

SARA: **Sort of.**

RUTH: **Sort of? What does "sort of" mean?**

SARA: **It means that we did go out to look for something.**

RUTH: **A dress? Where are you going to get the money to buy clothes?**

SARA: **No, we weren't looking for anything to wear.**

RUTH: **Well, then, where did you go?**

SARA: **Downtown. Over on Broadway.**

RUTH: **Broadway? What were you doing on Broadway? I've told you not to go over to Broadway.**

SARA: **It was something different. Exciting.**

RUTH: **What are you talking about? You aren't making any sense.** *(Silence)* **Are you going to tell me or not?** *(More silence)* **I'm glad you and Lisa didn't get hurt. Where did you two go?**

SARA: **Oh, Mother. I can't tell you anything. You never think I do anything right.** *(Exits into the kitchen.)*

RUTH: *(Following her)* **Wait a minute, young lady. We haven't finished our conversation!**

Read "Sara and Ruth," Take 2 as it has been edited. Note: (1) the stage directions at the beginning of the scene have been expanded; (2) Sara's actions described in the stage directions replace the dialog in the telephone conversation.

Because the audience does not know Sara's secret, the revised scene creates more suspense and more interest. As you

Because the audience does not know Sara's secret, the revised scene creates more suspense and more interest.

...stage directions may suggest the characters' feelings and allow the author to write fewer lines of dialog.

read the rest of this revised scene, read the stage directions closely. Notice the way stage directions may suggest the characters' feelings and allow the author to write fewer lines of dialog.

SARA AND RUTH: TAKE 2

(A living room. SARA, 18, pops her head in from the kitchen door, looks around, and then disappears for a moment. When she reappears, she is walking quickly. Carrying a medium-sized cardboard box, she crosses to the center archway, peeks down the hall, then tiptoes quickly up the stairs. After a moment of silence, we hear the Off-stage sound of a key turning in the latch. Next we hear the door open. RUTH, a woman in her early forties, dressed in work clothes, enters. Exhausted, she walks slowly into view and calls toward the kitchen.)

RUTH: Sara! Hi, Sara! *(Pause)* You making dinner? *(No answer. RUTH moves to the stairs.)* Sara! You upstairs, honey? *(Pause)*

SARA: *(Off-stage, upstairs. In a somewhat forced cheerful voice)* Hi, Mom!

RUTH: Thought you said you'd make dinner if you got home ahead of me. *(She sinks wearily onto the sofa.)* Whew! I worked my tail off today.

SARA: *(Runs down stairs.)* I just got home myself. I'll go start dinner. *(She heads for the kitchen quickly.)*

RUTH: *(Absentmindedly)* Did you study at Lisa's house for your science test? It must have taken a long time. You should have been home hours ago.

SARA: *(Stops.)* Well, we talked for a while, then we got bored. So Lisa and I went for a ride in Lisa's car. *(Continues toward kitchen.)*

RUTH: Where did you go? *(SARA stops.)* Did you go shopping? *(RUTH is tired. She doesn't want to talk. She just wants to change into a robe.)*

SARA: Sort of. *(Looks down at the floor, away from her mother.)*

RUTH: *(Impatiently)* Sort of? What does "sort of" mean?

SARA: It means that we did go out to look for something.

RUTH: *(Not really paying attention to SARA)* Clothes?

SARA: No, we weren't looking for anything to wear. *(She begins to inch over toward the kitchen, away from her mother.)*

RUTH: Well, then, where did you go?

SARA: Downtown. Over on Broadway.

RUTH: Broadway? *(Her voice and temper begin to rise. This is a subject they have talked about before.)* **I've told you not to go over to Broadway.**

SARA: **It was something different.** *(SARA wants to tell her mother but is still afraid.)* **Exciting.**

RUTH: **What are you talking about? You aren't making any sense.** *(She struggles to her feet and heads for the stairs, muttering to herself.)* **Broadway.** *(Once there, she turns.)* **I'm glad you and Lisa didn't get hurt. Where did you two go?** *(Silence)*

SARA: **Oh, Mother. I can't tell you anything. You never think I do anything right.** *(Then, with a burst of energy)* **I got a kitten at the Humane Society.** *(She rushes into the kitchen.)*

RUTH: *(Surprised and speechless)* **A what?!** *(Suddenly realizing what SARA just said, RUTH races quickly toward the kitchen.)* **You come back here right now, Sara!**

ACTIVITY #9

Making Your Actions Speak Louder Than Words

Purpose of Activity #9

Each student (1) will gain experience writing stage directions; (2) will delete at least three lines of dialog; and (3) will learn to edit and make changes in his/her script.

DIRECTIONS

Edit *one* of your three scenes. Add five stage directions and remove at least three lines of dialog.

1. Read aloud the two "Sara and Ruth" scenes in Activity #8. Next, reread the scenes that you have created. Now select *one* of the scenes that you wrote that you like best.

2. Begin to "polish" this scene. Try to change some of the "telling" that you have done by adding actions which "show." Your characters may imply or hint at an idea rather than state it out loud. Consider movement and emotions in your stage directions. Some characters may reveal their feelings by their actions. Your major objective is to make a good scene even better.

3. Suggest appropriate dramatic actions through stage directions. Plays are built on dramatic action. An

Consider movement and emotions in your stage directions. Some characters may reveal their feelings by their actions.

audience often learns as much from the manner in which lines are delivered as it does from the actual words spoken.

4. Include the "Seven Characteristics of a Good Scene" (below) in your revision. Activity #9 represents your most carefully edited writing. Your instructor may give this assignment a separate grade.

Seven Characteristics of a Good Scene

• Write opening stage directions which establish a setting and a mood.

• Write natural sounding dialog.

• Write helpful stage directions which suggest a character's feelings or state of mind.

• Write clear character traits revealed through dialog.

• Create a central conflict.

• Create a clear crisis and resolution (or a suggestion of a future resolution).

• Show evidence of hard work and thought when this scene is compared to an earlier scene.

UNIT THREE SUMMARY

After participating in The Playwriting Game: Storyboard, *you learned that writing an outline for a play can be enjoyable.*

Activity #9 is the last official assignment. As the title indicated, this unit was an introduction to playwriting. The purpose of each activity was to make you comfortable and familiar with the early stages of playwriting. After participating in *The Playwriting Game: Storyboard* you learned that writing an outline for a play can be enjoyable.

In this unit you have learned:

1. The vocabulary of a playwright.

2. The structure of a traditional play.

3. The form for writing a script.

4. To write lines of dialog.

5. To edit your scripts.

6. To write stage directions.

7. To share ideas and to help others create their scripts.

These skills provide a good foundation for future playwriting. They are important building blocks. The word *playwright* actually means *play builder*. May the plays you build in the future serve as beautiful homes for the stories you have to tell.

UNIT THREE EVALUATION GUIDELINES

1. Completed *Storyboard* Summary Sheet after finishing
   Game 1 of *Storyboard*. (10) _____

2. Completed Activity #4. (15) _____
   Had twenty lines or more of dialog.
   Included basic elements of dramatic plot.
   Turned in work on time.

3. Completed Activity #6. (15) _____
   Had twenty lines or more of dialog.
   Included basic elements of dramatic plot.
   Seemed more "polished" than Activity #4 scene.
   Turned in work on time.

4. Completed Activity #7. (15) _____
   Had twenty lines or more of dialog.
   Included basic elements of dramatic plot.
   Seemed more "polished" than Activity #4 scene.
   Turned in work on time.

5. Completed Activity #9. (15) _____
   Wrote opening stage directions, created a central conflict, clear crisis,
   and a resolution.
   Turned in work on time.

6. Participated in at least one writers' response group. (10) _____

7. Showed leadership by helping others and sharing scripts with the class. (25) _____

8. Arrived on time and worked hard with group during class. (10) _____

Total _____

60-69 = D,   70-79 = C,   80-89 = B,   90-100 = A,   101-115 = A+

NOTE
Theatre is a collaborative learning experience. The greatest number of points are given to students who work cooperatively with their group and who help others.

UNIT FOUR
Monologs

When you hear the word monolog, do you think of a comedian or talk show host? Comedians stand alone on-stage. They use monologs to "warm up" the audience and make them laugh. That type of monolog is the one you are probably familiar with.

The word monolog is a combination of two Greek words: *mono* meaning one and *logue* meaning speaker. So a monolog consists of lines delivered by one person. In a play, a monolog is a lengthy speech delivered by one of the characters. Other characters can be present during the scene. But only one actor speaks the lines.

Most plays do not have a narrator. Therefore, authors use monologs to explain facts to the audience. Without the monolog, viewers might not learn important details about a character's background, feelings, loves and hates. Play monologs may sometimes be comic. However, many monologs are serious. In either case, the actor delivers information to the audience.

In this unit you will learn to memorize and to perform a monolog from a play. Though you may be speaking to other characters on-stage, you will be in the spotlight. Your job will be to give "life" to a character through your voice, body, and an intelligent interpretation of a series of lines. By analyzing, memorizing, and performing a monolog, you will broaden your skills as an actor.

Memorizing. Does that word scare you? It shouldn't. You memorize facts, words, names and directions every day of your life. You have been memorizing since you were a very small child. So when it comes to memorizing some lines, you have nothing to worry about. Both the text and your instructor will suggest techniques that make the memorization process easier. Relax. You will be successful.

Without the monolog, viewers might not learn important details about a character's background, feelings, loves and hates.

ACTIVITY #1

A Sample Monolog

The following pages describe eight activities that will help you to prepare a monolog for presentation. Anyone can read a monolog to himself. You are going to read your monolog, understand it and then perform it. Furthermore, you will be successful.

To help explain each step, this chapter will refer to a monolog from the English play "Box and Cox." The speaker in the monolog is Mrs. Bouncer. Near the beginning of the play she has a few minutes alone on-stage.

The premise of the play is that Mrs. Bouncer is trying to earn extra money by renting the same room in her home to both Box and Cox. Mr. Box is a printer. He works during the night and sleeps in the room during the day. Mr. Cox makes hats. He works during the day and sleeps in the furnished room at night. Only Mrs. Bouncer, the landlady, knows that the two men live in the same room. Both men believe that their room is vacant when they are at work. The entire play takes place in the one room that both Box and Cox rent.

Purpose of Activity #1

Class members will listen to a student present a demonstration reading of Mrs. Bouncer's monolog so that they can understand the characteristics of a monolog speech.

DIRECTIONS

1. Listen closely to Mrs. Bouncer's monolog. Watch the performer as he/she delivers the monolog. Does the performer move? Does the performer change "voices"?

2. Think about the answers to the following questions as you watch and listen to the monolog.

   • Do you like the monolog?

   • Does it hold your attention?

   • What, specifically, do you like best about this monolog? Be prepared to give two examples.

   • Would you change anything about the manner in which the monolog was delivered?

- What would you do differently?

- Why would you do these things differently?

- Did the performer move around the "stage"?

- Would you, as the performer, move when you speak your lines?

- Does movement help to hold the audience's attention? Why or why not?

3. Your answers to these questions will help you to choose a monolog that you will enjoy performing.

Would you, as the performer, move when you speak your lines?

A Sample Monolog

MRS. BOUNCER: He's gone at last! I declare I was all in a tremble for fear Mr. Box would come in before Mr. Cox went out. Luckily, they've never met yet. And what's more they're not very likely to do so; for Mr. Box is hard at work at a newspaper office all night, and doesn't come home till the morning, and Mr. Cox is busy making hats all day long, and doesn't come home till night; so that I'm getting double rent for my room, and neither of my lodgers are any the wiser for it. It was a capital idea of mine — that it was! But I haven't an instant to lose. First of all, let me put Mr. Cox's things out of Mr. Box's way. *(She takes the three hats, COX's dressing gown and slippers, opens the door at L. and puts them in, then shuts door and locks it.)* Now, then, to put the key where Mr. Cox always finds it. *(Puts the key on the ledge of the door.)* I really must beg Mr. Box not to smoke so much. I was so dreadfully puzzled to know what to say when Mr. Cox spoke about it. Now, then, to make the bed — and don't let me forget that what's the head of the bed for Mr. Cox becomes the foot of the bed for Mr. Box. People's tastes do differ so. *(She goes behind the curtains of the bed and seems to be making it.)*

ACTIVITY #2

Finding a Monolog That You Would Like to Perform

Purpose of Activity #2

Students will learn how to locate a monolog that they would enjoy performing.

DIRECTIONS

1. Look at the monolog resource materials that your teacher provides in the classroom.

2. Choose a monolog that you like. Many catalogs offer high interest, short, easy to perform monologs. Choose one that you think is humorous or sad. Choose one that you would like to perform. Choose a monolog that suits *you* best. Everyone in the class has distinct tastes and personalities. Therefore, everyone may prefer different monologs.

3. Read the following section titled, "Five Suggestions for Finding the Best Monolog for You."

Five Suggestions for Finding the Best Monolog for You

> *Shorter monologs are easier to memorize and to perform. They also hold the attention of the audience.*

1. Choose a character from a play that you like and know something about. Select a monolog that is not too long. Shorter monologs are easier to memorize and to perform. They also hold the attention of the audience.

2. Choose a monolog that talks about problems, fears, worries, loves, or family matters relating to your age. Or you may prefer a humorous monolog.

3. Look at children's plays like "Cinderella," "Snow White," or plays adapted from Dr. Seuss books. There will be monologs for both females and males.

4. Compare the length of the speeches as well as their content. If you are concerned about memorizing the words, choose a *short* monolog of interest to *you*.

5. Look for soliloquies. Soliloquies are speeches delivered by a character who is alone on-stage. Shakespeare's tragedies contain many famous soliloquies. In Elizabethan times audiences believed that a character was expressing his inner thoughts when he was alone on-stage.

   In modern plays, soliloquies are sometimes spoken by characters who are also the "narrator." Frequently these narrator/characters begin the play by talking directly to the audience. Many children's plays have narrators.

   Four plays using narrator soliloquies are: "The Glass Menagerie," "The Skin of Our Teeth," "Teahouse of the August Moon," and "Zooman and the Sign."

ACTIVITY #3

Developing a Clear Interpretation of Your Monolog

In Activity #3 your goal is to discover the "tone" of your speech. You want to understand the feeling or attitude that the character is trying to express. You want to hear how the speech "sounds."

At first, you may feel foolish reading the monolog out loud so many times. But the process is not silly. It makes perfect sense. You are going to present the piece out loud, therefore, that is the way you should practice it from the start. Your voice is a key tool. Learn how to use it well. Practicing your monolog out loud is an aid to memorization. Right now, do not worry about memorizing lines. You will be learning them naturally as you practice.

Purpose of Activity #3

Through practice, students will develop a clearer understanding of their monologs.

You now have selected a monolog. You think to yourself, "How do I begin?" You will take it step by step.

DIRECTIONS

1. Read the speech aloud six or seven times. Stand up. When you stand as you speak, you have more energy.

2. Read the *entire* monolog out loud during your first three readings. Do not worry about how "good" your interpretation is.

3. Experiment with the *rate* in which you speak. Slow down your speech or speed it up. *Emphasize* different words within a sentence.

4. Listen for sentences that seem to sound "right." Try to duplicate that interpretation when you read the piece again.

5. After three readings, listen for sentences that do *not* sound "right." In those instances, stop. Go back and read the previous two sentences. Then read the one that is not sounding right.

   • Vary your pitch. Make it high; then make it low.

   • Change the speed in which you deliver your lines.

Vary your pitch. Make it high; then make it low.

• Ask yourself questions about the character who is speaking: Why is the character saying this sentence at this time? Has her mood changed? Her motive? Is she now talking to somebody else or to herself?

ACTIVITY #4

Asking and Answering Questions About Your Monolog

Now that you have a clearer understanding of your monolog, what do you do next? You need to ask and answer some questions about your monolog. You probably have already begun to ask yourself questions. Now you will find out if you know the answers relating to your monolog. Once again, Mrs. Bouncer's monolog is used as an example in order to explain the answers to each of the questions.

Students will better understand their monologs by asking themselves questions about the monolog.

Purpose of Activity #4

Students will better understand their monologs by asking themselves questions about the monolog.

DIRECTIONS

1. Answer the following questions about your monolog.

Question 1: Ask yourself: Who is the character talking to in my monolog? Is there somebody else on-stage or in the wings? Is he talking to the audience? To himself?

Sample answer 1: In the selection from "Box and Cox," Mrs. Bouncer is alone on-stage. She appears to be talking both to herself and to the audience. She appears to be a chatty, friendly neighbor. She is trying to explain to the audience why she is picking up Mr. Cox's personal items and locking them in a closet out of sight.

Question 2: Ask yourself: What does my monolog reveal about my speaker's personality and state of mind? What is his mood? What tone of voice is implied? Does the mood stay the same or does it change? Does it change several times?

Sample answer 2: Mrs. Bouncer is a clever, energetic, organized businesswoman. She cleans the room after each man leaves for work so that neither Mr. Box nor Mr. Cox knows that anyone else is staying in the room. Furthermore, she makes the bed one way for Mr. Box and another way for Mr. Cox.

Underline any words in Mrs. Bouncer's speech that indicate her personality. Can you think of any other adjectives to describe Mrs. Bouncer? Is she nervous? Is she hardworking? Is she creative?

Question 3: Ask yourself: Are there words in my monolog that I can't pronounce or don't know the meaning of? Are there complete sentences that I can't quite figure out? Why did the author use these words? Why did he include these sentences?

Sample answer 3: Sometimes there are strange words in monologs. Often they are "old-fashioned" words. Other words are simply ones with which we are not familiar. The stage directions refer to Mr. Cox's dressing gown. What is a dressing gown?

Question 4: Ask yourself: Does my monolog suggest an item that the performer might use as a costume or prop? Is a setting mentioned? Are any colors suggested? Do stage directions provide any clues?

Sample answer 4: How do you think Mrs. Bouncer is dressed? This play is over one hundred years old. What do you think a landlady might wear? Would she wear anything on her head? If yes, what? Would she wear an apron? A long dress? What type of shoes? How do you think the room might look? Mrs. Bouncer refers to Mr. Box's three hats, a dressing gown, and slippers. Mr. Box smokes. Therefore, in his locked closet there must be an ashtray.

Question 5: Perhaps the most important question you need to ask is: Why has the author included my monolog in his/her play?

Sample answer 5: Mrs. Bouncer's speech is useful for the author. The writer quickly explains the premise of his play to the audience. The play is a comedy and Mrs. Bouncer sets the tone for the audience.

Perhaps the most important question you need to ask is: Why has the author included my monolog in his/her play?

Finding answers to questions will help you to make convincing use of your voice, body, facial expressions and gestures. Continue practicing your reading out loud. Remember: You are going to present the piece out loud. Therefore, that is the way you should practice it.

ACTIVITY #5

Practice, Practice and More Practice

After completing Activity #4, you are beginning to feel good about your monolog presentation. You have been practicing out loud. You have been asking questions about why the character moves a certain way. You may even have decided on a costume for the performance.

Purpose of Activity #5

Students learn to present their monologs successfully by practicing vocal interpretation, movement, gestures, interpretation of the lines, and memorization techniques.

DIRECTIONS

Use facts about your character's personality to determine your movements and gestures.

1. Continue to work on vocal interpretation. Begin to concentrate on your movement and gestures. Use facts about your character's personality to determine your movements and gestures.

2. Use props and interact with the audience. Does your character begin the monolog as a narrator? If so, make eye contact with the "audience" as you practice; or direct your gaze off-stage if that is where you imagine the "listener" is located; or imagine other characters on-stage. You may want to use a chair to represent a person sitting and listening to the character's story.

3. Experiment with your movement and voice changes. The movements and voice should *reveal the feelings* of your character. If the character is worried, let your voice show it. Try lowering your voice at appropriate places. Try raising your voice at other times. Variety in voice tone, loudness and speed make your monolog more interesting to the listener.

   Your movement can be broad or sharp. For example, you might stroll across the acting area or you might make a quick turn. Your movements can also be tiny, like stroking your chin with your thumb and forefinger in a thoughtful pose.

   In Mrs. Bouncer's monolog from "Box and Cox," the actor could bustle around busily and then stop briefly from her duties to look at or talk directly to the audience.

4. Keep repeating your lines over and over again. Repeating lines helps you to memorize. *Repetition* also helps to remind you to change your voice and movements as you speak. You will feel comfortable with your lines, movements and voice inflections as you experiment with your monolog.

5. Listen to your lines as you say them. *Listening* to the lines helps you to remember them. You are already memorizing. You probably know whole sections by heart. How did you learn them? You learned them by repetition. You repeated your lines, motions and special voice changes. Talking out loud has many advantages. One is that you can hear the words.

6. Focus on your *interpretation* of the lines. Are you using any props? Do you use hand gestures? Do you move about the "stage"? If so, you may find that the script is becoming a nuisance. Soon you will want to memorize the whole speech. Then you will not have to worry about the script.

Repeating lines helps you to memorize. Repetition also helps to remind you to change your voice and movements as you speak.

A MEMORIZING TIP THAT REALLY WORKS

Memorize only three lines at one time. Once you know those lines, memorize another three lines. Repeat all six lines. Next, memorize an additional three lines. Repeat all nine lines. Repeat this process until you have memorized your entire monolog. Remember: It is easier to memorize information in small segments.

ACTIVITY #6

Practice Makes Perfect

Think of a favorite song. Now think about the part that is repeated over and over throughout the song. Lines that are repeated are called the refrain. Do you know why the writer repeats those lines? He wants the listener to memorize them quickly. The songwriter wants you to remember the words. He wants you to sing them. He also wants you to buy the record!

Purpose of Activity #6

Each student will memorize the words in the monolog by repeating the lines over and over again.

DIRECTIONS

1. Like the refrain in a song, repeat your monolog over and over. Continue reciting out loud. Remember the memorizing tip on page 65.

2. Put the finishing touches on your character's stage movements. Decide where you are going to stand as you speak. These stage decisions are called blocking.

   You now have more knowledge about your character. Therefore, you can block movements quickly. Put the finishing touches on your character's stage movements by adding gestures. These gestures can indicate a change in mood or motive when the character begins to speak key sentences.

3. Work with a partner.

   • Your partner can sit "on-stage." He can react as if he is the person to whom you are speaking.

   • Or your partner can be an observer in the "audience." You decide which arrangement will serve your needs best. Your partner can play the role of "fellow artist." He can provide positive feedback after you have finished your reading.

   • A partner will encourage you. He/she will offer praise and positive suggestions and comments. A good partner will also tell you which parts of the reading may be unclear.

4. Be a good listener to your partner. You will learn from helping your partner with his/her monolog.

   • Avoid general statements such as: "I liked your characterization a lot," or "Your reading was very good." These sentences do not give the actor specific details or suggestions.

   • Give specific suggestions. That means, tell your partner exactly what you liked. For example, you might say: "I laughed when you rolled your eyes just before you said, 'Why can't she leave me alone?' It was just the right gesture for a girl that age to make."

   • Practice making positive, helpful comments. For example, you might change a critical comment into a positive question. "Was there a reason that you turned your back to the audience when you crumpled

Be a good listener to your partner. You will learn from helping your partner with his/her monolog.

the letter? I didn't understand what your character was thinking at the time." Criticism is not appropriate for this activity.

- Give specific helpful examples to your partner. The comment above points out a single moment in the reading. That comment is more helpful than a statement like: "You had your back to the audience a couple of times."

- Develop your skills as a communicator. As you observe and listen to your partner, you will improve your own monolog. You also will have the pleasure of encouraging another person to become a better actor.

ACTIVITY #7

Polishing Your Performance

The deadline for your first "public" performance is almost here. Are you a little nervous? Most people get nervous before any type of public speaking. In fact, most professional actors get the "jitters" before a performance. However, like the professionals, you will do just fine. Why? Because you have practiced your craft of acting.

Most people get nervous before any type of public speaking. In fact, most professional actors get the "jitters" before a performance.

Purpose of Activity #7

Each class member will polish his/her monolog presentation by practicing the monolog out loud.

DIRECTIONS

1. Begin to "polish" your performance. Good organization and practice produce a good performance. You can and will be successful in your performance.

2. Select the parts of your monolog that need more polish. If you have not memorized all your lines, set aside time to do that now. An actor must know his lines by heart in order to be in control of his performance.

3. Ask a friend, parent, sister, or brother to help you memorize your lines. Remember: Only memorize three lines at one time. Once you have learned the three lines, memorize three additional lines. Then repeat all six lines out loud.

> **Work on voice variations, eye contact, pauses, timing and facial expressions if your memorization is perfect.**

4. Continue to practice your monolog out loud. Repetition helps memorization.

5. Work on voice variations, eye contact, pauses, timing and facial expressions if your memorization is perfect.

6. Choose the props that you will be using in your actual performance. Locate a costume. Have everything ready now. Do not leave these decisions to the last minute; you may not be able to find exactly what you need on the day of your performance.

7. Decide today how you wish to handle props and use your hands.

ACTIVITY #8

Making the Presentation

When the day comes for you to perform your monolog before an audience, you may experience butterflies in your stomach. You may ask yourself, "Am I really ready? Is there anything else I should have done?" There are a few last-minute details you need to consider.

Purpose of Activity #8

Each student will perform a monolog.

DIRECTIONS

1. Read the following eleven suggestions for successfully performing your monolog.

2. Decide which suggestions will help you create a smoother performance.

3. Practice your introduction out loud.

ELEVEN SUGGESTIONS FOR A SUCCESSFUL MONOLOG PRESENTATION

1. Clothing: Decide what you are going to wear. People who are prepared are successful in life. Make sure that your costume or the "outfit" you have chosen is ready and in order. A dark or all-black ensemble forces viewers to focus on the character.

2. Introduction: Plan your introduction now. In many cases your teacher will tell you how to announce your memorized selection. If you are given no guidelines, consider the following introduction:

Hello. My name is _____, and I will be performing a monolog from the play _____, which was written by _____. I am playing the part of _____.

Briefly, you may want to give background information leading up to the beginning of your monolog.

3. Rehearse the introduction several times before your performance. You gain self-confidence when you are comfortable on-stage. You will be comfortable on-stage if you practice your entrance.

4. Use one of the actors' "tricks" for beginning a monolog.

- Some actors momentarily turn their backs to the audience. They relax their shoulders. An actor may keep his head down. He may make a few adjustments in his costume, then slowly he turns back toward the audience — in character.

- Others face the audience. They bow their heads. They concentrate for a few moments, and then look up in character.

- Still others may take a seat. They "freeze" into a still pose. Then they break the pose with the first words of the monolog.

If you prepare other monologs in the future, watch fellow actors as they perform. You will learn new ways to introduce a performance.

5. Be well-prepared. You want your audience to know that you are self-confident. You will be self-confident if you are prepared.

6. Plan and rehearse your initial walk across the stage to downstage center.

- Keep your shoulders squared but not stiff.

- Hold your head high.

- Look at the audience.

Be well-prepared. You want your audience to know that you are self-confident. You will be self-confident if you are prepared.

- Pause when you arrive at center stage. Take time to make eye contact with all the members or sections of your audience.

7. Speak with assurance. Have a pleasant expression on your face.

8. Throughout your monolog, continue to make eye contact. Look directly into every person's eyes. Look to the left. Look center. Then look to the right.

9. Speak loudly enough so that all listeners can hear you. Your tone of voice and your bearing should be sending a message: "You are going to like this monolog."

Smile. Relax...Give yourself a moment to feel "at home" on-stage.

10. Smile. Relax. Look at everyone again. Give yourself a moment to feel "at home" on-stage. This is important. The butterflies will begin to go away.

11. Conclusion: Finally, decide how you will conclude your performance. The simplest way to end is to pause for a few seconds after delivering the final line. Then, turn toward the audience. Bow your head. Then, after a two-second pause, raise your head. Gracefully acknowledge any audience applause. Confidently walk off-stage.

You did a great job!

UNIT FOUR SUMMARY

You've completed your monolog. Congratulations! Preparing a monolog well requires much thought and practice.

In Unit Four you have learned:

1. Self-discipline.

2. To read analytically.

3. To analyze and interpret your lines.

4. To memorize.

5. To ask questions about your character.

6. To reveal information through vocal inflection and movement.

7. To concentrate on pitch, volume, voice control and voice variations.

8. About blocking movements.

9. To add appropriate gestures.

10. To experiment with appropriate costumes and props to enhance your reading.

11. To overcome stage fright.

12. To provide feedback to fellow learners.

These skills are not only useful on the stage; they can help you succeed in school and on the job.

Take another bow.

UNIT FOUR EVALUATION GUIDELINES

MEETING DEADLINES

1. Completed Activities #2, #3, #5 and #7 on time.   (20) _____

2. Memorized monolog by Day Seven and took
   pride in doing quality work.   (25) _____

3. Arrived on time ready to work with partner.   (10) _____

COLLABORATIVE TEAM EFFORT

4. Accepted offers of help from team members, worked hard and
   helped others on team.   (30) _____

5. Offered help to partner and provided cooperative support.   (30) _____

                                                         Total _____

70-79 = C   80-89 = B   90-100 = A   101-115 = A+

NOTE

Theatre is a collaborative learning experience. The greatest number of points are given to students who work cooperatively with their group and who help others.

EVALUATION GUIDELINES

Your teacher will use the same evaluation form for this unit as she used for the storytelling unit. This form, reprinted below for you to preview, will be used to rate your performance. Your instructor may also ask you to consider each category in order to provide feedback to other classmates. In addition, your teacher will use the Unit Four Evaluation Guidelines that assess teamwork. They are printed on page 72.

Theatre Class
Performance Evaluation

Name _____

Project _____

	EXCELLENT (4)	GOOD (3)	FAIR (2)	POOR (1)	NONE (0)
MEMORIZATION, PREPARATION					
MOVEMENT, BLOCKING					
CONCENTRATION					
ARTICULATION, DICTION					
PROJECTION					
EXPRESSION, CHARACTERIZATION					
RATE OF SPEECH					
POISE, STAGE PRESENCE, APPEARANCE					
ENERGY, CREATIVITY					
OVERALL EFFECT					
READY ON TIME					
Subtotals					
Total					

UNIT FIVE
Introduction to Puppetry

Did you ever see a puppet show when you were young? Did you ever have an opportunity to make a puppet in school? No one is too old to enjoy puppets. Puppets can do, say, and be anything you wish them to be. Puppets give pleasure to everyone — the person who watches them and the person who creates them.

Puppets give pleasure to everyone — the person who watches them and the person who creates them.

This unit gives you the opportunity to combine many of your theatre skills. Puppetry expands your expertise in: (a) character creation and development; (b) voice control; (c) improvisation; (d) playwriting; (e) costuming; (f) storytelling; (g) monologs; (h) blocking; (i) simple set design; (j) staging; (k) stage terminology; (l) entering and leaving the stage area; (m) working cooperatively as a group to achieve a finished product; (n) rehearsing; and (o) creating a final product for a performance.

However, you will also accomplish something even more important. You will bring joy to youngsters, fellow students, older adults or anyone watching your puppet show.

ACTIVITY #1
Let's Make Puppets

Purpose of Activity #1

Each class member will create one or more puppets for use later in a puppet show.

DIRECTIONS

1. Each student will follow the directions for making "The Quick and Easy One-Piece Puppet." A one-piece puppet has a head, body and arms.

2. Create this puppet by gluing together two pieces of felt material. Felt material is preferred because it is thicker and retains its shape.

THE QUICK AND EASY ONE-PIECE PUPPET

Materials

- Two pieces of a solid-color felt material — 22" x 10"
- A piece of cardboard 2½" x 3"
- A hot glue gun
- "Tacky" glue or Elmer's Glue
- A needle and thread
- Small scissors
- Cotton balls

> **NOTE**
>
> Your teacher will provide many of these items. She also has a "class share box." Students are encouraged to exchange ideas and to share supplies with one another.

Students are encouraged to exchange ideas and to share supplies with one another.

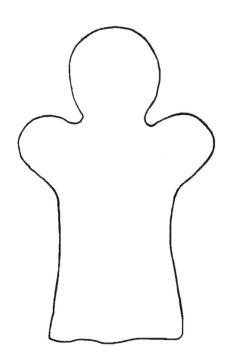

Activity #1 — Illustration 1

Procedure

1. Your teacher will give you a pattern for "The Quick and Easy One-Piece Puppet."

2. Trace this template onto two pieces of felt material. Use a solid color. Later in Activity #11, you will decorate your puppet with pieces of plaid, prints, ribbon, sequins, or anything you wish.

3. Cut out the two pieces of felt material.

4. If there is a difference between the "right" side of the fabric and the "inside" of the fabric, place the two "right" sides facing each other. You will be working on the side of the fabric that will not be seen. It will be the inside of the puppet once it is completed.

5. Using a hot glue gun, glue the two sides, the neck and head of the material together. If you prefer, you can hand sew the two pieces of material together. Leave the bottom of the fabric open. You need to place your arm and hand inside the puppet body.

6. After you have glued (or stitched) your material on three sides, turn the puppet inside out. Now you will see the "right" side of the material. The side that you glued (or stitched) will be hidden. After completing your gluing, stuff the head of the puppet with cotton balls.

7. (a) Cut out a piece of cardboard 2½" x 3" and form it into a tube. This tube will be the sturdy "neck" of your puppet.

   (b) Leave one inch of the tube showing underneath the head.

   (c) After you have created the neck for your puppet, take the neck out.

   (d) Fold and adjust the cardboard for your fingers. You may want to use only your pointer finger in the neck of the puppet or two fingers: the pointer and middle fingers.

   (e) Hot glue the sides of the neck tube together. Then place the tube back into the neck of the puppet.

8. Leave the puppet body plain. Later, after you write your puppet play and you know the characters, you will decorate the puppets appropriately with: ribbon, lace, leather, glitter, sequins, beads, buttons, macaroni, yarn, feathers, scraps of material and/or fabric paint.

...after you write your puppet play and you know the characters, you will decorate the puppets appropriately...

NOTE

Experiment using different fingers in the head of your puppet as well as the arms. Your pointer finger usually goes inside the puppet head. The thumb and third fingers are placed inside the arms of the puppet. You may wish to practice using other fingers that are more comfortable for you. Practice moving your puppet's head and arms to determine which fingers are best for you.

PUPPETEER TIP: As a puppeteer, you need to wear a dark, long-sleeved shirt when working with puppets, or find an old pair of men's dark socks or women's dark knee highs. Cut off the feet. Next, put the socks on your arms as a sleeve. In this way, no skin will show. You want the attention directed to the puppets — not to the puppeteer.

ACTIVITY #2

Making Puppets Move

Each class member will learn the standard hand positions and how to make their puppets move believably.

Purpose of Activity #2

Each class member will learn the standard hand positions and how to make their puppets move believably.

DIRECTIONS

1. In groups of four, students will practice the standard hand positions for Exercise #1. Your teacher may provide additional suggestions and exercises.

2. In Exercise #2, students will practice moving their puppets more believably. Students remain in their small groups. Continue this exercise until you are comfortable moving your puppet naturally. Students are encouraged to help one another and offer suggestions.

3. In Exercise #3, students rehearse their pantomimes in pairs. However, they will "perform" these pantomimes alone. The pantomime will consist of three separate puppet movements.

EXERCISE #1
Standard Hand Positions

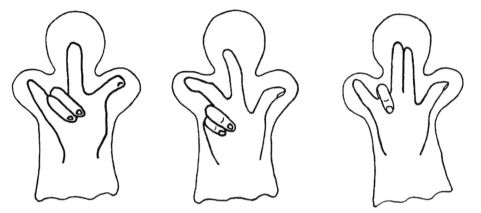

Activity #2 — Illustration 1

EXERCISE #2
Making Your Puppet Move Believably

Directions

Working in groups of four, students practice these warm-up activities one at a time.

1. Have your puppet wave hello or good-bye.

2. Have your puppet shake its head "yes" and "no."

3. Have your puppet bend over and pick up an object. (Movement should come from the wrist.)

4. Have the puppet throw out its hands to indicate surprise.

5. Have your puppet clap its hands.

6. Make the puppet look embarrassed or shy.

7. Have your puppet walk on and off the stage. (Move your arm up and down to create the effect of walking.)

EXERCISE #3
Puppet Pantomimes: Three Movements

Directions

Students rehearse in pairs but perform alone. Create pantomimes which consist of three separate movements. Then ask the class to guess what you are doing in each movement.

Procedure

Following are four sample pantomimes. You may wish to create your own.

1. Look for an object, pick it up and then show surprise.

2. Walk in, fall down, then show you are sad.

3. Crawl into the "room," look around to see that no one is following you. Then stand and run off.

4. Sit down, stand up and wave wildly to someone.

ACTIVITY #3

Making Puppets Speak

Every puppet must have a distinct and appropriate voice. To find which voice is suitable for your puppet character, you must experiment.

Every puppet must have a distinct and appropriate voice. To find which voice is suitable for your puppet character, you must experiment. There are four ways in which you can change your voice. You can change the *tone, pitch, volume* and *speed*. Each puppet should have a distinct sound in each of these areas.

TONE: angry, sad, happy, frightened, surprised, confused, elated

PITCH: high, low, medium

VOLUME: loud, soft, medium

SPEED: fast, slow, medium

Purpose of Activity #3

Each class member will learn the methods for making puppets speak. Unlike regular acting, a puppeteer often may have to exaggerate the tone or pitch of the puppet's speaking voice.

DIRECTIONS

1. Practice changing tone, pitch, volume and speed using familiar children's tales.

2. Exaggerate your voice and movements as a puppeteer.

3. Students read aloud the Exercises #1, #2, #3, #4 and #5. The entire class participates as a group in the first four exercises. Each of these exercises will help you to develop your puppet's tone, pitch, volume and speed.

EXERCISE #1:
Developing Your Own Unique Tone

The class is divided into two groups.

Group #1 portrays the wolf in *The Three Little Pigs*. They will practice, in an *angry* tone, the line: "Little pig, little pig, let me in!"

Group #2 portrays the pig. They will practice, in a *frightened* tone, the line: "Not by the hair of my chinny chin chin!"

EXERCISE #2:
Developing Your Own Unique Pitch

The class is divided into two groups.

Group #1 is Papa Bear in *Goldilocks and the Three Bears*. They will practice, in a *low* voice: "Someone has been eating my porridge!"

Group #2 is Baby Bear. They practice, in a *high* voice: "Someone's been eating my porridge and has eaten it all up!"

EXERCISE #3:
Developing Your Own Unique Volume

The entire class can be the voice of the giant in *Jack and the Beanstalk*. They will practice, in a *loud* voice: "Fee, fie, fo, fum. I smell the blood of an Englishman!"

EXERCISE #4:
Developing Your Own Unique Speed

The entire class can be the voice of *The Gingerbread Man*. They will practice, in a *fast*, but clear voice: "I'll run, I'll run as fast as I can. You can't catch me! I'm the Gingerbread Man!"

Reading and saying aloud familiar lines is a great way to practice tone, pitch, volume and speed. For more practice, choose additional lines from tales. Whenever you practice any skill, you become more proficient and successful.

Reading and saying aloud familiar lines is a great way to practice tone, pitch, volume, and speed.

EXERCISE #5:
Speaking in Your Puppet Voice: Improvisation

ROUND ONE: Now that you are comfortable with your new "voices," you are ready to practice short scenes. Once again, students will work in pairs. Each pair will improvise brief passages from favorite children's stories. Possible suggestions include: *The Three Little Kittens, Snow White, The Three Billy Goats Gruff, Little Red Riding Hood, Chicken Little, The Ugly Duckling,* and *Rapunzel.* One person will play one role. The partner will play another. For example, one puppet can be the mother cat in *The Three Little Kittens.* The other puppeteer can be the kitten(s). Or one puppeteer can be Little Red Riding Hood. The other puppeteer can play the wolf.

ROUND TWO: Students work in pairs. Each pair will switch roles and practice the other person's part emphasizing tone, pitch, volume and speed.

ROUND THREE: Each puppeteer will appear alone on the puppet stage with his/her puppet. Practice speaking for the puppet. You do not need a real puppet stage. You can use any type of partition.

Students can take a large piece of cardboard and cut a rectangle near the top. Place this cardboard "stage" on a desk. Sit behind the cardboard and position your puppet in the rectangular opening. Puppeteers are inventive and creative. You do not need a lot of money or elaborate equipment to be a good puppeteer.

First, each student will introduce his puppet behind the "puppet stage" or partition. The puppet should walk to center stage, turn to the audience and say, "Hello, my name is _____. I am unique because _____."

You can then ask the puppet several questions. The puppet should respond by using complete sentences.

ACTIVITY #4

Learning the Basic Rules of Puppetry

Review the following basic, common sense puppetry guidelines before you begin more complex improvisations. Remember that professional puppeteers started just where you are starting. Professionals learn and practice the same rules.

Purpose of Activity #4

Each student will learn the basic rules of puppetry by reading them and using them in their puppet plays.

Remember that professional puppeteers started just where you are starting. Professionals learn and practice the same rules.

DIRECTIONS

Students take turns reading aloud the following six basic rules.

Puppets are like actors in a play. They walk on and off the stage. They do not pop up or disappear suddenly unless there is a reason.

1. Puppets are like actors in a play. They walk on and off the stage. They do not pop up or disappear suddenly unless there is a reason.

2. Puppets should stand at a three-quarter position so the audience can see their faces.

3. Puppets should move their heads or make some kind of gesture to indicate they are speaking.

4. The puppets that are listening should freeze.

5. A puppet should speak in a loud, clear voice and one which is appropriate to his character.

6. Puppets should move up, down, and forward to create a walking movement.

ACTIVITY #5

Puppetry Improvisations

Purpose of Activity #5

Each class member will learn the methods for making puppets move and speak naturally and believably. Students will practice the basic rules of puppetry from Activity #4.

DIRECTIONS

1. Working in pairs, students select topics A-H (below) to improvise as a short skit. Make sure that your skit has a beginning, a middle and an end.

2. Any of the skits can be adapted for three puppet characters.

A. One puppet is a professional male or female basketball player. The other puppet is a shy child who wants to shake the basketball player's hand or get an autograph.

B. One puppet is a burglar who is entering a darkened home. The other puppet is a second burglar entering the same house through a separate window. The burglars do not know each other.

C. One puppet is a lost mouse looking for her family. The other puppet is a hungry fox (or cat) who claims that he/she wants to help the mouse find her family.

D. One puppet is a mother preparing dinner. The other puppet is her son or daughter. He/she has something important that he/she wants to tell the mother.

E. One puppet is a visitor from a foreign country who knows only four English words or phrases: "No, thank you," "ham and eggs," "water," and "Where is the bathroom?" The other puppet is a waiter/waitress in a diner.

F. One puppet is a lion tamer in a circus. The other puppet is a lion.

G. One puppet is a mad scientist who wants to blow up the world. The other puppet is a "right-minded" superhero who must stop this mad scientist.

H. One puppet is a grandmother. She is beginning to have trouble remembering simple things. She does not want her children or grandchildren to know what is happening. The other puppet is her grandchild who has come to visit.

ACTIVITY #6

Choosing the Audience for Your Puppet Play

Purpose of Activity #6

Each class member will participate in choosing an audience for a simple play for puppets.

DIRECTIONS

You may want to write one play for youngsters, one for junior high students and one play to be performed for older adults.

1. Students will choose the audience for whom they are writing: Are the viewers older adults? Children, six to eight years old? Ten to twelve years old? Teens? You may want to write one play for youngsters, one for junior high students and one play to be performed for older adults.

2. Working in groups, students read aloud the questions from the following section, "Selecting an Audience."

SELECTING AN AUDIENCE

A. Will the audience be a grade school class? If so, what age and grade is the audience?

B. Will the audience be a junior high school class? Or will you choose a nursery school group?

C. Knowing the age and interests of your audience before you begin writing will help you to write a better play.

Selecting a Topic

Knowing the age and interests of your audience before you begin writing will help you to write a better play.

Purpose of Activity #7

Students will choose a topic for their puppet plays which is appropriate for the age of their audience.

DIRECTIONS

1. Working in their groups, students read aloud the following questions. You do not need to answer them at this time.

   • Are you writing a play for younger children? They like plays in which the characters are animals. Young children also like humorous plays.

   • Are you writing a play with a certain message? For example, "Just say no to drugs."

   • Are you writing about being proud of yourself?

   • Are you writing a puppet play that deals with death?

   • Are you writing a puppet play for older adults? Older adults enjoy humor. You can talk about most subjects as long as you inject humor.

   • Are you writing a puppet play for junior/senior high school students that deals with divorce?

   • Are you writing a puppet play about friendships?

   • Are you writing a puppet play that deals with family problems?

2. Read the following three categories. Your group may wish to select a topic from these examples or your group may wish to create its own topic.

A. FAMILY TOPICS:

1. Biggest problem with: parents, sisters and brothers
2. Biggest fight with: my parents, cousins, sisters, brothers

B. FRIENDSHIP TOPICS:

1. Friend who moves away
2. Friend who dies
3. Best things about good friends
4. Biggest fight with best friend
5. One main problem with best friend
6. Biggest worry about friend

C. FEARS AND WORRIES TOPICS:

1. Fear of making mistakes
2. Fear of being left out by other kids
3. Fear that people will make fun of you
4. Fear of certain kids in school
5. Fear of death (death of parents, grandparents, a pet, yourself)
6. Fear of old age
7. Fear of failure in school, sports, or friendship
8. Fear of separation from friends, parents, relatives
9. Fear of illness
10. Fear of drugs
11. Fear of parental or adult abuse
12. Fear of crime: robbery, beating, murder
13. Worries about physical appearance
14. Worries about school
15. Worries about parents or grandparents
16. Worries about divorce

ACTIVITY #8

Guidelines for Writing Puppet Plays

Students learn the guidelines for writing successful puppet plays.

Purpose of Activity #8

Students learn the guidelines for writing successful puppet plays.

1. Working in groups, students read out loud the "Six Guidelines for Writing Puppet Plays."

2. Each team applies these guidelines as they create their puppet play.

SIX GUIDELINES FOR WRITING PUPPET PLAYS

1. For a class program, write several short plays rather than one lengthy one. Each play should have two to four characters. More than four characters often causes confusion and problems behind the puppet stage or simple partition.

2. Student written plays should be approximately five to seven minutes in length.

3. A good script is a simple one, having only a few scene changes.

4. The same principles for writing a standard play apply to a puppet play: have a good conflict and lots of action!

5. Create dialog that is flexible. Your characters' lines should allow the puppeteers the opportunity to improvise ideas rather than to memorize many lines.

6. Show the scripts to your teacher before your group begins to rehearse. Make sure that the language, plot and costumes are appropriate for the age of the audience.

A good script is a simple one, having only a few scene changes.

ACTIVITY #9

Writing a Puppet Play

Purpose of Activity #9

Working in teams, students will write a puppet play.

1. Students will create their plays and dialog based on the topics in Activity #7. Limit the number of characters to three or four. Difficulties arise when there are more than four puppeteers behind a partition at one time.

2. Students will read and apply the "Six Guidelines for Writing Puppet Plays" as they create their plays.

3. Students will show their scripts to their instructor before the group begins to rehearse. Make sure that the language, plot and costumes are appropriate for the age of the audience.

ACTIVITY #10

(Optional)

Storytelling With Puppets:
Choose a Tale or Children's Story
Use Puppets to Tell Stories From Long Ago

Although puppeteers frequently write their own plays, they also tell favorite stories from long ago. When you tell stories from memory, you are practicing the age-old custom of storytelling. The same procedures that you practiced in the Storytelling Unit in this *Theatre Arts 2 Student Handbook* are ones that you would use now for your puppet play.

Purpose of (optional) Activity #10

Students will choose a tale or children's story. Students will tell this story using puppets as the speakers.

DIRECTIONS

1. Read the following section titled "Five Suggestions for Using Puppets in Storytelling."

2. Apply the suggestions in your puppet storytelling performance.

FIVE SUGGESTIONS FOR USING PUPPETS IN STORYTELLING

Focus the attention of the audience on your puppets. Your puppets are the center of attention — not you.

1. Focus the attention of the audience on your puppets. Your puppets are the center of attention — not you. Even if you do perform without a stage, the attention of the audience will still be on your puppets.

2. Have your puppets dress, move and "talk" in appropriate voices. Just as you would change pitch, tone and volume in regular storytelling, so will your puppets change voices during the course of a tale.

3. Practice your storytelling with your puppets and puppet

voices. Practice makes perfect in any type of storytelling. Make certain that you know the story well and can tell the story with feeling and understanding.

4. Practice your puppets' movements so that they are natural but dramatic. Exaggerated movements can be seen and understood better on-stage than smaller, indefinite gestures. Exaggerated but clear dramatic puppet voices also command audience attention. Dramatic voices help the audience to understand the dialog and follow the story more easily.

5. Share your gift of storytelling and puppetry. Your audience will love your performance.

Share your gift of storytelling and puppetry. Your audience will love your performance.

ACTIVITY #11

Completing Your Puppet:
Creating Facial Features, Hair and a Costume

Purpose of Activity #11

Class members will complete their puppet faces and bodies. Puppets will reflect the characters in the puppet plays or stories.

MATERIALS

Anything can be used to create eyes, hair, hats, crowns and costume decorations.

- a hot glue gun
- magic markers
- scraps of material
- buttons
- ribbon
- leather pieces
- sequins
- macaroni and different shapes of pasta
- feathers

- "tacky" glue
- felt material
- yarn
- fabric paint
- lace
- glitter
- beads
- any craft and sewing trim items

NOTE

Your teacher will provide many of these items in the class "share box." Students are encouraged to exchange ideas and to share supplies with one another.

DIRECTIONS

1. Ask a neighbor or relative who sews if they have any scraps or trim materials that they would give you for your puppet.

2. Bring a paper bag to class filled with trim items that you have collected and a small pair of scissors.

3. Look at the drawings of sample puppets that were created from "The Quick and Easy One-Piece Puppet" pattern. These drawings are printed at the end of Activity #11. You can create any type of puppet: (a) animal puppets (b) adult puppets (c) children puppets (d) monster puppets (e) older adult puppets (f) teenage puppets, or (g) famous people puppets.

4. Your instructor will give you templates for making: (a) a bird beak, (b) a duck bill, (c) dog and bunny ears, (d) cat ears, (e) a tongue, and (f) moose antlers. Each pattern is provided only as a suggestion. You may wish to draw and use your own patterns.

5. Follow each of the following steps. (a) Cut the templates into separate pieces. (b) Pin the pattern pieces onto a piece of felt material or a piece of cardboard. Felt material is thick and sturdy and holds its shape well. (c) Cut the facial pieces. (d) Use a hot glue gun to affix the ears, eyes, mouth, or antlers to the puppet head. (e) If you wish, form your eyes, nose or mouth out of felt, buttons, pasta pieces, or any other materials from the share box.

6. Yarn can be used for hair. (a) Cut pieces of the yarn and glue them to the head with the hot glue gun. (b) Next, create any decorations that you wish to place over the hair: headband, crown, scarf, ribbon, beads, or flowers. (c) Glue these decorations to the puppet head.

7. Share ideas with teammates. Working in groups helps generate creativity. You may find that you have a great idea for someone else's puppet. Or they may have an idea for your puppet. Sharing materials and ideas will make this activity on puppetry more enjoyable. Use your imagination!

Share ideas with teammates. Working in groups helps generate creativity.

PROCEDURE: CREATING A PUPPET
FACE AND PUPPET HAIR

1. To create a simple eye, cut two ½" circles of bright felt. Using a hot glue gun, glue the circles for eyes onto the puppet head.

2. Cut two smaller circles of black, brown, blue, red, or purple felt. Glue these circles over the larger circles. You now have two simple eyes.

3. Or: (a) glue two buttons onto the head for the eyes; or (b) glue two pieces of circular pasta for eyes.

4. Create a nose, mouth, ears or beak by gluing the materials you have chosen onto your puppet's head.

5. Use yarn, ribbon or felt to create the appropriate hair for your puppet. Be creative. All people and animals do not look alike. Create a beautiful unique puppet.

All people and animals do not look alike. Create a beautiful unique puppet.

Activity #11 — Illustration 1

Activity #11 — Illustration 2

Activity #11 — Illustration 3

Activity #11 — Illustration 4

PROCEDURE: CREATING AN APPROPRIATE COSTUME

Trim your puppet's "costume" body with appropriate decorations for your puppet's character, whether the puppet is an animal or a person.

1. Trim your puppet's "costume" body with appropriate decorations for your puppet's character, whether the puppet is an animal or a person. For example, (a) if the puppet character is an animal or human grandmother, give the puppet a shawl or "sweater"; (b) if the puppet character is a human or animal rock star, create a fancy, glittery costume; (c) if the puppet is merely a dog character, make a plain dog's body with a tail; and (d) if the puppet is a human or animal monster, create your puppet costume with felt scraps, fabric paint and trim.

2. Use any of the items from the share box to create your puppet costume.

3. Reminder: As a puppeteer, you need to wear a dark long-sleeved shirt when working with puppets, or find an old pair of men's dark socks or women's dark knee highs. Cut off the feet and put the socks on your arms as a sleeve. In this way no skin will show. You want the attention directed to the puppets — not to the puppeteer.

ACTIVITY #12

Presenting the Puppet Play

Purpose of Activity #12

Each class member will participate in presenting a puppet play. Students will practice the basic rules of puppetry from Activity #4.

DIRECTIONS

1. As a group, class members will take turns reading aloud the following section titled, "A Checklist: Steps to Complete Before Beginning Rehearsals."

2. Students read out loud the section titled "Rehearsing the Play."

3. Continue reading aloud "The Final Touches Before the Performance."

4. Begin to rehearse your puppet play.

5. Present your play before a small audience.

A CHECKLIST:
Steps to Complete Before Beginning Rehearsals

1. Have you completed your puppets?

2. Can you move your puppet comfortably?

3. Have you adequately practiced the tone, pitch, volume and speed voice exercises?

4. Do you know your parts? Have you memorized your lines?

5. Have you (or your teacher) blocked the play?

   • Each puppeteer has a definite place to stand or kneel behind the puppet stage.

   • Each puppet has a definite position on the stage.

6. Read the following five rules of "puppetry manners" as practiced by professional puppeteers:

   • No talking among puppeteers behind the stage unless it is part of the play.

   • No puppet appears before his cue.

   • No puppeteer peeks out from under the curtain.

   • Puppeteers remain behind the puppet stage until the performance is over.

   • After the play is over, the puppeteers come out and take a bow with their puppets.

REHEARSING THE PLAY

Rehearsing for a puppet play is similar to rehearsing any play. The differences have been covered in the checklist and in the sections on voice and movement. Now you will concentrate on memorizing your lines and moving and speaking at the appropriate time.

Remember: (1) Your class either wrote this play or selected a favorite old tale to retell. Successful puppet plays are generally short and simple. Therefore, you will have fewer lines to memorize. (2) Your audience will be either young or elderly. Either way, they will love your play. That does not mean that you do not have to do a great job. It just means that you do not have to be nervous. Your audience is eager to see your play. They want you to be successful. (3) Do not over-rehearse. Often three or four class rehearsals are sufficient for a short play. Make this puppetry experience fun as well as educational!

Your audience is eager to see your play. They want you to be successful.

THE FINAL TOUCHES
BEFORE THE PERFORMANCE

Scenery

1. Scenery can be painted on a polyester curtain with tempera or acrylic paint. Keep it simple. Be precise in your work. Sloppy work can detract from the show.

2. Scenery pieces can be cut out of cardboard and held up with magnetic tape, popsicle sticks, or by other puppeteers.

Music

1. Use music that is appropriate to the mood of the play. It can be taped and played at the beginning and end of the show. Marches and folk dance music are effective for introducing a show.

2. You may wish to use live music, such as a kazoo, castanets, and harmonica, drums, a tambourine, triangles or a piano.

Sound

Nothing is worse than to work hard on a show and have the audience unable to hear you!

1. Remember! The audience must be able to hear you. Speak loudly. The viewers must hear your words if they are to pay attention and understand your play. Nothing is worse than to work hard on a show and have the audience unable to hear you!

2. Are you using any sound effects? If so, you will need to locate and bring a tape recorder or disc player to class. Your instructor may have a tape recorder for you to use.

Lighting

1. Most likely, your group will not need special lighting. Your team is performing a simple puppet play for a small audience.

2. If necessary, for classroom performances, use two photographer clip-on lights: one on each side of the puppet stage.

Good luck! Break a leg! Happy puppeteering!

UNIT FIVE SUMMARY

This chapter on puppetry challenges you to use many skills you have learned in other areas of theatre education: improvisation, playwriting, storytelling, monologs, voice control and inflection. The puppet play called for group collaboration: (a) play production, (b) scene blocking, (c) rehearsing, (d) set design, and (e) the creation of the puppets themselves.

Preparing any play requires cooperation, patience, perseverance, and practice.

Congratulations! You've completed your puppet play. Preparing any play requires cooperation, patience, perseverance and practice.

In Unit Five, you learned:

1. To create a basic one-piece puppet.

2. To create appropriate facial features, hair, costume decorations, hats, shawls and props for your particular puppet character.

3. To make puppets move and speak believably.

4. To develop your own puppet voice.

5. To follow basic puppetry guidelines.

6. To improvise scenes using puppets as characters.

7. To write short puppet plays.

8. To use storytelling with puppet characters.

9. To block a puppet scene.

10. To choose appropriate props.

11. To create simple scenery.

12. Stage terminology like Stage Left, Stage Right or a three-quarters position.

13. The appropriate puppetry manners used by professional puppeteers.

14. To present a finished puppet play for small audiences.

UNIT FIVE EVALUATION GUIDELINES

The student completed "The Quick and Easy One-Piece Puppet."   (15) _____

The student learned to make puppets move and
speak believably.   (10) _____

The student learned and used the basic rules of puppetry
outlined in Activity #4.   (10) _____

With a partner, the student successfully performed an improvised
puppet skit.   (15) _____

With his/her team, the student wrote a play for puppets.   (15) _____

The student completed the facial features, hair and appropriate
costume decorations for his puppet.   (15) _____

The student enthusiastically participated in the final presentation
of a puppet play before an audience.   (15) _____

The student arrived on time, worked cooperatively in his/her group,
and helped others complete their work.   (20) _____

Total   _____

60-69 = D,   70-79 = C,   80-89 = B,   90-100 = A,   101-115 = A+

NOTE

Theatre is a collaborative learning experience. The greatest number of points are given to students who work cooperatively with their group and who help others.

EVALUATION GUIDELINES

Your teacher may use an adapted performance evaluation form for this unit to assess your puppet performance. The form may be similar to the following one from Unit Two. Your instructor may also ask you to consider each category in order to provide feedback to other classmates.

Theatre Class
Performance Evaluation

Name _____

Project _____

	EXCELLENT (4)	GOOD (3)	FAIR (2)	POOR (1)	NONE (0)
MEMORIZATION, PREPARATION					
MOVEMENT, BLOCKING					
CONCENTRATION					
ARTICULATION, DICTION					
PROJECTION					
EXPRESSION, CHARACTERIZATION					
RATE OF SPEECH					
POISE, STAGE PRESENCE, APPEARANCE					
ENERGY, CREATIVITY					
OVERALL EFFECT					
READY ON TIME					
Subtotals					

Total

UNIT SIX
Designing an Interior Set

Why do magicians fascinate us? Probably because they make us see things that are not really there. We know that the magician has not really sawed a body in two. Or do we? The person in the box certainly looks as if his body is in two pieces. There is nothing but empty space between the assistant's hips and his legs. How does the magician do it? He creates an illusion. Everything he does is just pretend.

When you think about it, theatre is also an illusion. It is pretend. An audience goes to a theatre and watches performers on-stage. Members of the audience know that the performers are actors. They are not really the characters they are portraying.

The actors have taken on a new identity. They are characters living their lives before us in a room, park, battlefield, dungeon, castle, or building. If they are good actors, we honestly believe, for a few hours, that everything is real.

Theatre is a type of magic. During a magic show, the magician has several assistants. Actors also have many assistants who make their illusions "come alive."

Theatre is a type of magic... Actors have many assistants who make their illusions "come alive."

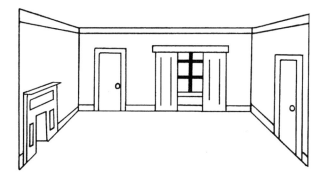

Illustration A — Interior Set

This chapter focuses on the magic created by set designers. Designers and technicians not only create a world of illusion for the audience; they also create a world of illusion for the actors. Set designers allow actors to believe in the roles they are creating.

Like other units in this course, Unit Six helps you to understand how artists collaborate. The entire production company works together to create the illusion of theatre. Everyone benefits from cooperation, especially the audience.

ACTIVITY #1

Learning the Vocabulary of a Set Designer

...the most common type of scenery made for plays is called a box setting.

The majority of plays are presented on **proscenium stages**. Most scenes in the plays take place in an interior setting. Interior sets are usually rectangular or box-shaped. Therefore, the most common type of scenery made for plays is called a **box setting**. This unit is about the creation of **box sets**.

Words like the ones in bold type above will be used throughout this unit. Other terms may strike you as "new" or strange as well. The following glossary is provided to help you with your reading. It will also help you when listening to stage technicians discuss their craft.

Purpose of Activity #1

Each class member will learn the vocabulary that set designers use. With the help of your instructor and through the process of learning to read a **ground plan** and construct a mini-model, you will learn the meaning of these terms.

DIRECTIONS

1. Read aloud the following section titled, "A Glossary of Stage Terms." Each of these terms is used by stage technicians, designers and directors. Most actors are familiar with these terms.

2. Discuss the words in the glossary. Ask questions about terms you do not know or understand. Do not be embarrassed if you have never heard these words. Many people do not use or even know these words.

A GLOSSARY OF STAGE TERMS

PROSCENIUM THEATRE: The most common type of theatre in western civilization. Seats in a **proscenium theatre** all face in the same direction. They face toward a raised stage at one end of the room. The stage is separated from the audience by a large plaster or wooden frame called a **proscenium**.

PROSCENIUM OPENING: The space that exists between the plaster walls that separate the stage area from the audience area in a **proscenium theatre**. Sometimes a speaker will say "proscenium" when he really means **proscenium opening**. The opening is often described by size: "The proscenium is twenty feet wide and eighteen feet high."

ARENA THEATRE: A type of theatre which has a stage in the center of the room. The audience surrounds the performers. The actors make entrances and exits down aisles in the seating area. The theatre buildings and the plays performed in them are also called **theatre-in-the-round**.

THRUST THEATRE: A theatre in which the audience surrounds a stage on three sides. Most of the acting is done on a large **apron** which thrusts out in front of the **proscenium**. The Globe Theatre in Shakespeare's time had a thrust stage. So do many newly built regional theatres in the United States.

GROUND PLAN: A blueprint-like sketch of a stage setting. It indicates the location of scenery on a stage floor. **Ground plans** are usually drawn to scale. They are one of the first drawings a designer makes.

DIRECTOR'S GROUND PLAN: A **ground plan** that the designer draws for the director to use. The director uses this plan for **blocking** the performance of a play. Blocking refers to the actors' movements on-stage. **Directors' ground plans** indicate the location and size of furniture on-stage. Labels and symbols on the sketch indicate that the plan is viewed from the perspective of an audience member.

Arena Theatre...a type of theatre which has a stage in the center of the room.

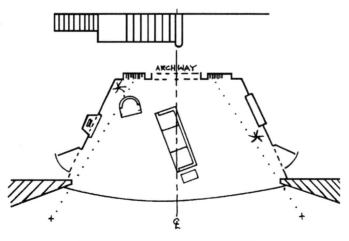

DIRECTOR'S GROUND PLAN
Activity #1 — Illustration 1

DESIGNER'S GROUND PLAN: A **ground plan** made for use by stage technicians. It is drawn from the point of view of the stagehand looking out toward the audience. It does not indicate the location of furniture. Often it will include notes about the length of walls and backings, and the height of any stairs or platforms that are part of the set.

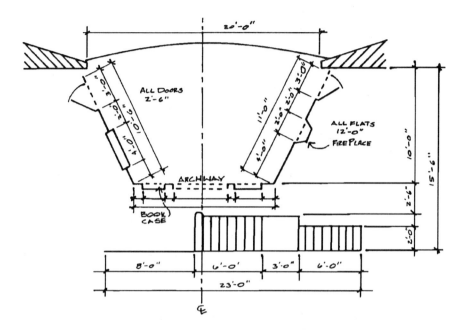

DESIGNER'S GROUND PLAN
Activity #1 — Illustration 2

Elevations for the scenic artist outline the size of a flat. They indicate the layout of whatever design must be painted on it.

ELEVATIONS: Scale drawings which indicate the size and shape of individual pieces of scenery that will be used in a stage setting. Some elevations are drawn for the stage carpenter. These indicate how the scenery should be constructed. **Elevations** for the scenic artist outline the size of a flat. They indicate the layout of whatever design must be painted on it.

RENDERING or **SKETCH:** A perspective drawing which shows what the designer imagines the finished setting will look like. It also indicates the mood it will create. **Renderings** are sometimes done in pencil. However, more often, they are sketched in watercolors or pastels. They aid the designer in communicating with the director, scenic artists, and other stage technicians.

MODEL: A three-dimensional representation of a stage setting. The walls are usually measured to scale. Then they are cut out of cardboard, balsa wood, or poster board and glued together. Some designers like to build models and paint or decorate them instead of drawing a sketch.

STUDY MODEL: A model which is unpainted but built to scale. The designer builds it to make certain that design features will fit the theatre space, and it will look fine when built full scale. A **study model** is sometimes called a "white model" because it is unpainted.

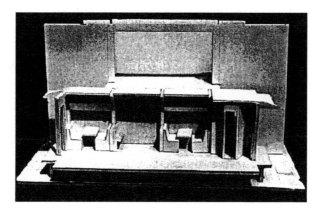

A STUDY MODEL
Activity #1 — Illustration 3

INTERIOR SETTING: A stage setting which depicts a room inside a house or other building.

BOX SET: An interior set with three walls. The fourth wall is imagined. It is left off so that the audience can see into the room.

FOURTH WALL: An imaginary, invisible wall. See **box set** above.

EXTERIOR SETTING: A stage setting which depicts an outdoor scene — a wooded area, a backyard, or a street corner.

SIMULTANEOUS SETTING: An arrangement of scenery which shows more than one room on the stage at the same time. A **simultaneous setting** may also show a combination of an **interior** and **exterior set**. Sometimes **set pieces** are placed in front of other scenery or background draperies. This is done so as to suggest one or more separate locales. For example, a table and chairs placed on the **apron** of a stage may represent a restaurant, while in the background the scenery reveals a bedroom.

SET PIECE: A single piece of scenery like a doorway, fireplace or a throne. They are placed on-stage to indicate a more

The fourth wall is imagined. It is left off so that the audience can see into the room.

elaborate setting. **Set pieces** are often used with one-act plays or for short scenes of longer plays which require several set changes.

APRON: The area of the stage floor closest to the audience. In a **proscenium theatre** it is the part of the floor that juts out in front of the main curtain. In a **thrust theatre**, it is the main acting area.

CYC or **CYCLORAMA**: A tall curtain or solid plaster wall at the back of a stage that is usually light blue. It represents a sky backing. **Cyclorama** curtains sometimes curve around to the sides of the stage. With proper lighting they can help designers create special effects such as an all red background, a sunset, or a moonlit night sky.

FLAT: A piece of scenery created by stretching muslin or canvas over a wooden frame. Usually, several flats are joined together. They form the wall of an **interior set**. If the wall is supposed to contain a door or a window, then a door flat or a window flat is used.

> *Cyclorama curtains sometimes curve around to the sides of the stage.*

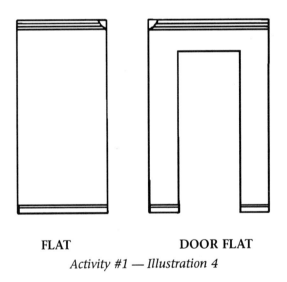

FLAT   DOOR FLAT

Activity #1 — Illustration 4

Flats may vary in width and height. However, the ones that are saved and reused are all a common height.

STOCK SCENERY: A collection of **flats**, doors, platforms, step units and other standard pieces of scenery. Stored backstage, these pieces are used over and over again for different plays.

HEADER: A piece of scenery that hangs or is supported over the heads of performers on-stage. The piece of wall above an archway is sometimes called a **header.**

BACKING: One or more flats that are positioned behind a door or window opening. They indicate another room or an outdoor scene beyond the main setting on-stage. Sometimes a curtain may serve as a **backing**. (See **cyc** and **masking**.)

MASKING: Black material or a painted black **flat** that is placed at the sides of a set, behind an opening, or behind cracks to prevent an audience from seeing backstage areas.

STAGE JACK: A right triangular wooden brace. It is used behind scenery walls or single **flats**. It helps to steady them and to keep them upright.

STAGE BRACE: A specially made wooden pole. It hooks into other special stage hardware and is used to help anchor and support stage scenery.

TERMS USED FOR GROUND PLANS AND MODELS

SCALE DRAWING or DRAWN TO SCALE: A way of describing a **ground plan** or **model**. One that has been precisely measured so that one inch or a fraction of an inch represents one foot on the actual stage. The ratio is usually written at the bottom of a **ground plan** as follows: **Scale: ½″ = 1′.**

ARCHITECT'S SCALE: A ruler which designers use to make **scale drawings**. Different edges on the ruler are marked to represent one foot at different scales.

CENTER LINE: A vertical dotted line on a **ground plan**. It indicates the exact center of the stage floor. The center line is usually labeled with the symbol ₵.

CURTAIN LINE: A dotted line on a **ground plan**. It indicates where the front curtain on a **proscenium stage** would normally fall.

PLASTER LINE: A dotted line on a **ground plan** that some designers use instead of a **curtain line**. It is drawn across the **proscenium opening**. It indicates the precise location of the stage-side surface of the **proscenium** walls.

SIGHT LINE: A reference to what is visible to and what is cut off from the view of audience members who are seated to the extreme left and right of the theatre. Designers and directors avoid putting important entrances, props, or dramatic action in areas of a stage setting which are not visible to some audience members. Plus (+) symbols at the lower left and right of a **director's ground plan** are used to figure sight lines.

Designers and directors avoid putting important entrances, props, or dramatic action in areas of a stage setting which are not visible to some audience members.

S.R. and S.L.: Abbreviations for *Stage Right* and *Stage Left*.

These terms always refer to the "right" and "left" of a person standing on-stage facing the audience.

U.R. and U.L.: Abbreviations for *Upstage Right* and *Upstage Left*. *Upstage* is the area farthest from the audience. The area closest to the audience is called *Downstage*.

> *Upstage is the area farthest from the audience. The area closest to the audience is called Downstage.*

ACTIVITY #2

Learning to "Read" a Ground Plan

Purpose of Activity #2

Each class member will learn to "read" and understand the markings and vocabulary used on a ground plan which is a designer's drawing of a set.

DIRECTIONS

1. Divide into groups of five or six students.

2. Each group will receive a brief "quiz" about the drawings that appear on the following two pages.

3. Answer the questions as a group. Most of the questions use words that appear in the "Glossary of Stage Terms." Use this list to check the accuracy of your answers. Write the answers below each question.

4. Write three new quiz questions for your instructor after your team completes the quiz. Follow the instructions on the second page of your quiz.

Jim Burwinkel, a professional scene designer, crafted the following ground plan and elevations. They were created for the play *Frankie and Johnny in the Clair De Lune,* written by Terrence McNally and staged by the Theatre Project Company of St. Louis, Missouri. The photocopies on the next two pages have been reduced in size to fit the textbook page.

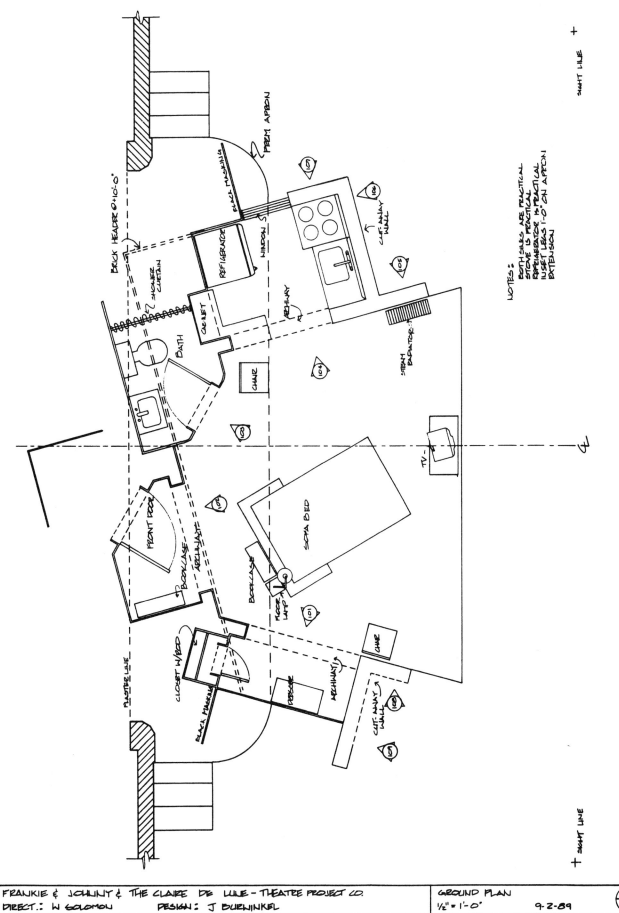

FRANKIE & JOHNNY & THE CLAIRE DE LUNE - THEATRE PROJECT CO.

DIRECT.: W GOLOMON   DESIGN: J BURWINKEL

GROUND PLAN

1/2" = 1'-0"   9-2-89

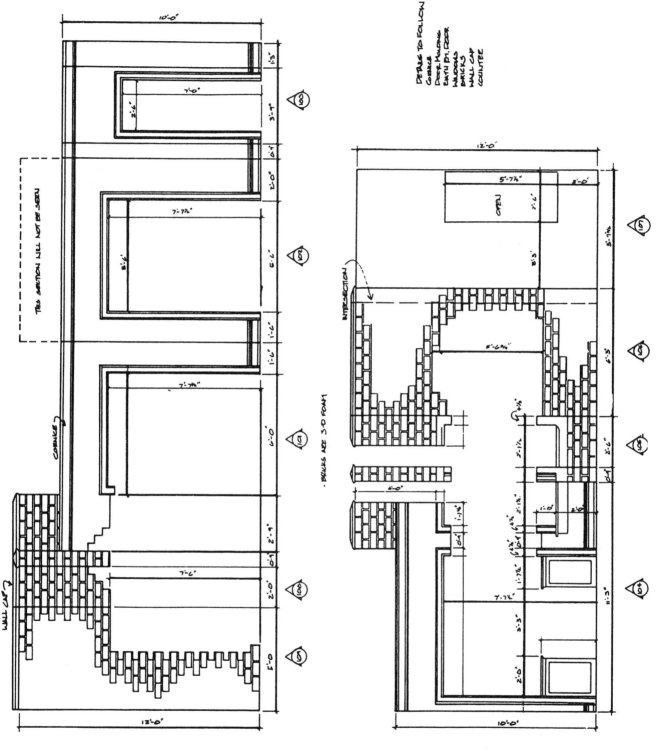

ACTIVITY #3

The Designer's View When Reading a Play

Activity #2 taught you how to read a ground plan. In Unit Six you are the set designer. Activity #4 will ask you to read and examine a brief play as a designer would read it. But how does a set designer read a play? The following paragraphs explain a set designer's view when reading a play.

Purpose of Activity #3

Students will understand the designer's unique perspective when he/she reads a play.

DIRECTIONS

1. Read paragraphs A, B, C, D, E and F.

2. Answer the questions on page 110.

A. The first time a set designer reads a play, he/she reads it for enjoyment. However, on the second reading, a designer begins to focus on lines and stage directions. Often, the lines directly state or give clues about the setting that the author imagined.

B. Frequently, an opening stage direction describes the setting in detail. Later in the script, other shorter directions may give more facts. Sometimes the author fails to mention these facts in the beginning. For example, if a stage direction says, "She opens a closet door, and a body falls out," the designer needs to have a closet door somewhere on-stage.

...if a stage direction says, "She opens a closet door, and a body falls out," the designer needs to have a closet door somewhere on-stage.

C. Actors' lines may also reveal: (1) the mood that a setting should create; (2) whether it is light or dark outside a window; (3) what season of the year it is; and (4) where a window should be located. The designer needs to be alert to these kinds of clues in a script.

D. The designer needs to consult with the director before starting the plans. Most directors have reasons for choosing a particular play. Directors know the effect they want the play to have on an audience. It is important that the designer understands and agrees with the director's concept. If there are areas of disagreement, they must talk them out.

E. The set designer reads the play a third time. He/she looks for setting clues that are not obvious. What design features help strengthen the director's concept? What props, wall hangings or other details show characters' moods or tastes? In view of what the director has said, what furniture should be removed or added? What feature or object in the room should be highlighted? Where should doorways be located?

F. At times the designer researches a play. The play may be set in another century. If so, the designer needs to learn about the furniture and decor of that time. If the setting takes place in a foreign country, the designer must read about fashions and architecture in that country. A designer might look for ideas in books which describe history, paintings, and successful scene designers of the past.

A designer might look for ideas in books which describe history, paintings, and successful scene designers of the past.

1. How does a set designer read a play for the first time?

2. What does the set designer focus on during a second reading?

3. How does the set designer know what the set looks like?

4. Does an author usually describe the set?

5. What other clues does the set designer look for in a play when he is designing a set?

6. Why does a set designer read a play a third time?

ACTIVITY #4

Reading the Play "Box and Cox"

Purpose of Activity #4

Students will read the play "Box and Cox" so that they can create a ground plan for the room that both Box and Cox rent.

DIRECTIONS

1. Read the play "Box and Cox" printed in the Appendix of this textbook. Read it once to enjoy and understand the humor.

2. Discuss the words and humor with your classmates. The play was written 150 years ago in England. Some of the old-fashioned words are strange. These words are footnoted and defined. You will not be tested on these words.

3. Read the play a second time. Take notes. What furniture must be present in the setting? Where do characters sit? Do they use chairs, a sofa, or a bed? Do they need a table? Windows? Does the action of the play call for more than one door? What rooms do various doors lead to? These questions are the same questions that Jim Burwinkel, a professional scene designer, asks himself before he draws a ground plan.

ACTIVITY #5

Making a Director's Ground Plan

Like an architect's blueprint, a ground plan is a scale drawing of the ground level space that a room will occupy. After reading a script carefully and talking to the director, the set designer creates a ground plan. A completed ground plan will serve as a guide to stage technicians and the play director. It is the first and most important drawing a set designer must make. Today you are the set designer.

Purpose of Activity #5

Working as a member of a team, students will make their own individual ground plans in class.

DIRECTIONS

1. Draw your own director's ground plan for the play "Box and Cox." Your plan will suggest a practical arrangement of walls, doors and furniture for the play. It should be drawn on a scale of ¼" = 1'.

   NOTE: Activity #6 will ask you to make additional ground plans. Therefore, read the following directions with care. Then apply them to Activity #6 as well.

2. Ask your teacher questions about anything that you do not understand. For this exercise, your teacher will play the role of the director. Remember: Directors choose plays for a reason. They often have a "vision" of what the scenery looks like. They also may have decided where they want key furniture or doors located. You, the designer, must consider the director's "vision" and his needs.

3. Get ready to play a game of "move the furniture, doors and windows around." You will create a ¼" scale ground

Directors choose plays for a reason. They often have a "vision" of what the scenery looks like.

> *Team members work together on their individual ground plans. Students help one another complete the activity.*

plan using everyday odds and ends.

4. Complete each of the following nine steps. Team members work together on their individual ground plans. Students help one another complete the activity. If you have any questions that your team cannot answer, ask your instructor to help you.

STEP #1: MATERIALS NEEDED

A copy of the play "Box and Cox" from the *Theatre Arts 2 Student Handbook,* and notes you have made about the play. The following materials will be supplied by your teacher:

- ¼" graph paper grid; on it draw a 20' wide proscenium opening.
- A book of paper matches with the tips cut off
- A well-sharpened pencil
- An eraser
- A pair of scissors
- A ruler
- A penny (or nickel), and
- Three or four thumbtacks or small shirt buttons

STEP #2: PREPARE YOUR MATERIALS

A. Tear out ten matches from the matchbook. Cut off and discard the heads. (Most likely, the tips from your match sticks will be precut.) Trim down each of the remaining stems to 1" lengths. These sticks stand for the 4' wide flats. They can be laid end to end to outline the walls of your box set.

B. Take two of the sticks and cut them in half. Now you have twelve pieces of matchsticks: eight 4' flats and four 2' flats. You are not going to use them yet. Keep them in a pile in a corner of your ground plan grid.

C. Now you are going to create some "furniture." Do you need a circular table about 3' in diameter? Use the penny. It is ¾" wide. In a scale of ¼" = 1', a penny can take the place of a 3' wide table. The head of a thumbtack shows the space most chairs would take up on a ¼" scale drawing.

If your matchbook cover is a standard size, it is 1½" wide. Cut off a ½" strip from the end. Now you have a piece of cardboard representing a sofa, 6' long and 2' wide. Trim it down if you prefer a love seat.

Activity #5 — Illustration 1

Cut off another strip 1" wide. Trim off ¼" from the long end of the resulting rectangle; you will have two pieces of cardboard. The small one might be a fireplace mantelpiece. The larger one can be a bed 4' wide and 5' long.

Activity #5 — Illustration 2

NOTE: Adult beds are over 6' long. However, on-stage, they are often shortened. This is done to provide more acting space. So 4' x 5' is a reasonable space to allow for a bed on a ground plan.

STEP #3: ARRANGE YOUR FURNITURE ON THE GROUND PLAN GRID

A. Make a list of furniture that you must have for the set. Look for items mentioned in the script, stage directions, or actor's lines.

B. Ask yourself, "What is the most important piece of furniture in the scene? Which piece should be the focus of attention?" Now place that object where you want it on the ground plan.

"What is the most important piece of furniture in the scene? Which piece should be the focus of attention?"

C. Put two other pieces of furniture next to the main piece of furniture. The position of each piece should make sense. For example, a chair near a desk, or a coffee table near a sofa.

D. Balance your furniture. Do you have a bed on one side of a room? Consider placing another heavy piece of furniture on the opposite side of the stage.

You are done — for the moment. Most likely you will move furniture before you finish. Therefore, do not worry about minor pieces of furniture yet.

STEP #4: ORGANIZE YOUR MATCHSTICKS

A. Pick up a matchstick and look at both sides. One side will be a gray, cardboard color. The other side will be coated with a white or black finish.

B. When the stick is placed on the ground plan with the gray side facing up, the match will represent a door flat.

C. Two gray sticks lying end to end will represent a double door or wide archway.

D. A matchstick with the finished side facing up will be a solid 4' wide flat.

E. Window flats or fireplaces can be created by writing a "W" or "F.P." on the surface of a match.

STEP #5: ADD PIECES OF THE WALL: DOORS AND WINDOWS

A. Decide how many doors you need. Where do you want to place them? Do you want an archway or double doors?

B. Are you placing doors in either the S.R. or S.L. wall? Then put a gray matchstick perpendicular to the proscenium wall where the "◊" symbol appears.

Do you want the door to be U.R. or U.L. on the side walls? Move the perpendicular matchstick five spaces straight up the page on the graph grid.

C. Doors in the back wall should be placed parallel to the curtain line. Put them along the graph line that is eleven spaces upstage of the curtain. These are temporary and approximate settings.

At this stage of planning, your set is a rectangular box with three walls and a proscenium opening.

D. Do you need windows or a fireplace? Do you want any? If so, where will they fit in sensibly? Experiment with several locations. Remember: At this stage of planning, your set is a rectangular box with three walls and a proscenium opening. You will need to put matchsticks end to end to create straight lines.

STEP #6: TIME TO ARRANGE THE FURNITURE AGAIN

A. Now it is time to consider the total picture. You may have to make changes.

B. Look at your ground plan. Try to imagine characters moving around furniture and in and out of doors.

Does any furniture block a door?

Would it be better to move a door to another place?

C. If you have to make changes, make them now.

D. Ask yourself:
   Where does each door lead?
   Which characters enter or go out of that door?
   Why do they use the door?

E. On your ground plan indicate which room or area is behind each door. Write that information lightly in pencil.

F. Look again at the movement of characters going on and off-stage and around furniture. Does everything make sense to you? If the answer is yes, then you are ready to add solid wall flats and to make final changes.

Look again at the movement of characters going on and off-stage and around furniture. Does everything make sense to you?

STEP #7: ADD SOLID FLATS NEXT TO DOORS, WINDOWS AND THE FIREPLACE

A. Pick up the matchsticks representing solid flats.

B. Place them end to end next to door, window and fireplace matchsticks to fill out a wall.

C. Angle in each side wall toward the back wall. The angle of the wall is no longer perpendicular to the proscenium wall. You angle in the side walls in order to keep more of the set within sight lines for most viewers.

D. Make sure that the downstage edge of each side wall begins at the "◊" symbol.

E. You may need to move the back wall closer in to the curtain line, or add short matchsticks representing 2' solid flats to the length of one or more walls.

F. With one or two changes, you can arrange the matchsticks into three straight lines. These three lines will make a pattern on the ground plan like one of the following diagrams.

Activity #5 — Illustration 3

STEP #8: DRAW YOUR GROUND PLAN TO SCALE

A. The final steps of this process are surprisingly easy.

B. Put a pencil dot at the point U.R. where the S.R. wall meets the back wall.

C. Put a second dot U.L. where the side and back walls meet.

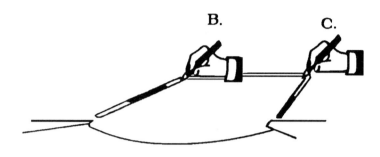

Activity #5 — Illustration 4

D. Now move the matchsticks away.

E. Using a ruler, draw a pencil line between the two dots. Next, draw a straight line between each dot and the nearest "◊" symbol.

F. You did it! You made a ¼" scale outline of the walls of your setting.

G. You will add doors and windows to the walls after you have drawn your furniture.

You did it! You made a ¼" scale outline of the walls of your setting.

STEP #9: ADDING THE FURNITURE AND FINISHING TOUCHES

A. Draw rectangles to represent various pieces of furniture.

B. Or trace the buttons, thumbtacks or coins you used to represent the furniture.

C. **Set Designer's Tip:** Show the way a chair is facing by tracing ¾ of the way around the tack. This shows the back of the chair. Then draw a straight line to indicate where the front edge of the seat is.

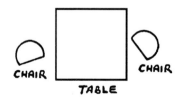

Activity #5 — Illustration 5

D. Write the name of each piece of furniture under it.

E. Erase sections of the lines that stand for the three walls. Next, indicate where you will place windows and doors. Expect that all windows and doors are 3' wide. You have been using ¼" scale. Therefore, 3' is ¾". The way to indicate doors and windows is shown below.

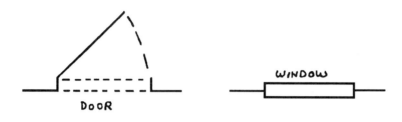

Activity #5 — Illustration 6

F. Do you want to show a fireplace? Look at the following diagram. Make the rectangle representing the mantelpiece ¼" wide and 1" long.

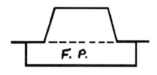

Activity #5 — Illustration 7

ACTIVITY #6

Creating Two More Director's Ground Plans

In Activity #6 you will make two more ground plans for "Box and Cox" by making two quick changes to your original ground plan. You may ask yourself why anybody would go to the trouble of drawing a second ground plan for the same play? It took a lot of time to make the first plan.

Two short answers might be: the first solution to a problem is not always the best one, and practice makes perfect.

Following are two reasons why set designers routinely create more than one ground plan for a play.

REASON #1: Trial and error helps everyone to see things in a new light. Set designers find fresh ideas when designing an alternative ground plan. For instance, a set designer may con-

Trial and error helps everyone to see things in a new light.

sider locating certain items in the plane of the fourth wall: an imaginary mirror, the hearth of a fireplace, or an umbrella stand. On the other hand, the designer might move furniture away from the walls so that actors can walk behind chairs or sofas. In fact, most set designers make an effort to place furniture away from the wall.

If a director is looking for more open space for the actors, the designer could use an archway Up Center to indicate a hallway beyond. One exit would suggest two separate areas off-stage (one to the right and another to the left). Many of these ideas may not have occurred to you the first time you created your ground plan. Drawing more than one ground plan is a challenge to your imagination.

REASON #2: Drawing alternative ground plans gives you practice making scale drawings. Like any manual skill, designing ground plans becomes easier each time you do it. You will find that altering an original ground plan takes less time than creating one. This unit gives sensible suggestions for adapting your ground plans. Each time you make one, you will discover your own shortcuts.

> *Drawing alternative ground plans gives you practice making scale drawings.*

Purpose of Activity #6

Working as a member of a team, each student will make two additional director's ground plans.

DIRECTIONS

1. **CHOICE #1:** During class, your teacher will discuss possible ways to adjust your design for "Box and Cox." Incorporate the changes described by your teacher into your two new ground plans.

2. **CHOICE #2:** Make the following two easy changes to your original ground plan. When you complete each variation, you will have created your two additional ground plans. It's that simple!

Easy Change 1: Reverse the details of your side walls. If a window was located in the center of your S.R. wall, put it in the S.L. wall instead. Exchange the location of doors as well. These changes may make it necessary to move your furniture around also.

Easy Change 2: Try to make a fancy set simple or a plain set fancy. Remove an unneeded window or piece of furniture, or use the archway idea mentioned on the previous page to indicate two off-stage areas with one exit.

(a) Is the room in your first ground plan too simple? Think of ways to improve it.

(b) Should you add a fireplace?

(c) A decorative table?

(d) A bookcase?

You did it. You made two or more easy changes to your original ground plan. You will agree that making changes to a ground plan is easier than creating the original plan. You are finished with Activity #6.

You will agree that making changes to a ground plan is easier than creating the original plan.

Discussing Ground Plan Alternatives

After you have completed your second and third ground plans, your instructor will provide class time for you to discuss your favorite plan with classmates. Be prepared to explain why you like one ground plan better than the others. You should be able to answer some other basic questions about that ground plan. These questions are printed below.

Purpose of Activity #7

Each student will discuss his/her ground plan changes.

DIRECTIONS

1. Gather with the entire class after completing Activity #6.

2. Sit with your teammates.

3. Share your ideas and changes with your classmates. Your instructor will ask team members the following questions about their ground plans. If you do not know an answer, a team member may provide one for you. You have done a great job.

(a) What do you like most about your arrangement of doors, windows and furniture?

(b) Where would characters be sitting or standing at the opening of the play? Or through which door would they make their first entrance? Why?

(c) Which piece of furniture (or other set decoration) might best characterize the mood of the room or the taste of its owner? The actual mood-setting detail may not be visible in the ground plan; it may merely exist in the mind of the designer.

ACTIVITY #8

A Mini-Model You Can Make in Minutes

QUESTION: How do you know what your set is going to look like? (a) Is the set supposed to be cheerful or depressing? (b) What colors will best express the feeling of the set? (c) Will the walls be a solid color? (d) Would wallpaper be better? (e) What style of furniture should we use? (f) How fancy should the woodwork around doors and windows be?

ANSWER: You are going to build a mini-model right on top of the final ground plan that you select. Then you will know what the set will really look like. Once you build the tiny walls, you can draw doors, windows, moldings, a fireplace, and other decorations on them.

Purpose of Activity #8

Working as a member of a team, students will make their own mini-models in class.

You are going to build a mini-model right on top of the final ground plan... Then you will know what the set will really look like.

DIRECTIONS

1. Read aloud the following fifteen steps for Activity #8.

2. Ask your instructor any questions you may have about each step. Every question is important. Remember: Once you begin working with your group, many of your questions will be answered.

3. Working as a member of a team, follow the fifteen steps for constructing a mini-model. Each student will build his/her own mini-model with the help of teammates.

4. Team members are expected to help one another complete each step before they move on to the next step. In that way, no one will fall behind and no one will be confused. Group work is not "cheating." Students learn from each other. Students discover new ideas from collaborative learning. Students are evaluated on their teamwork as well as their own efforts.

This model is easy to make. It may take longer to read the following directions than to make the model. Please read carefully. Follow each step of the directions in the order they are listed. Each step is short and fast.

STEP #1: Gather your materials.

(a) Your ¼″ scale ground plan for "Box and Cox"

(b) A pencil and eraser

(c) A legal size (9½″ x 14¾″) manila folder (which you will cut up)

(d) A pair of scissors

(e) A roll of transparent tape

(f) A ruler

(g) A right triangular straight edge (which can be cut from a piece of the manila folder)

(h) An X-acto or utility knife

STEP #2: Place the ground plan on your desk so that you are facing the set from the "audience."

STEP #3: Take the manila folder. Remember: You are still using a ¼″ scale. Therefore, a 2½″ wide strip of folder material will represent a 10′ high wall.

(a) Place the folder face down on your desk.

(b) Place your ruler along the left edge of the folder.

(c) Measure 2½″ above the centerfold.

(d) Make a pencil mark at the edge of the folder.

(e) Make a similar mark ¾″ below the centerfold.

(f) Repeat these steps on the right edge of the folder.

(g) Draw two horizontal lines connecting the marks at each edge.

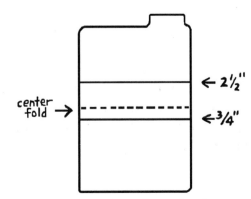

Activity #8 — Illustration 1

This model is easy
to make. It may
take longer to read
the directions than
to make the model.

STEP #4: Cut along the two pencil lines you have drawn. You will use the strip with a fold in it. Put aside the other two large pieces of folder for now. Look at the 2½" section of the folder above the centerfold. It will become your model walls. The ¾" strip will be used to attach the pieces to your ground plan.

STEP #5: Place your 2½" wall section face down on top of your ground plan. The ¾" strip stands upright. See diagram below.

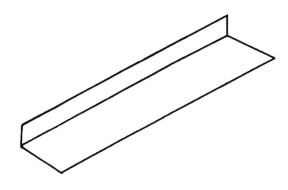

Activity #8 — Illustration 2

STEP #6: Place the whole strip along the line on your ground plan which represents the right wall of your set. Put the bottom right corner of your manila strip at the D.R. edge of the "wall."

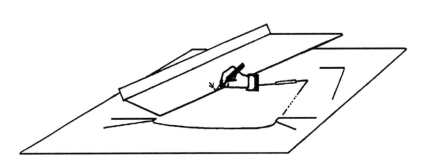

Activity #8 — Illustration 3

STEP #7: Make a pencil mark on the manila strip where it touches the U.R. corner of the right wall. Next, turn the manila strip around. It now runs along the length of the center "wall" (as it is shown in the ground plan). The U.R. corner should still be next to the mark on the strip.

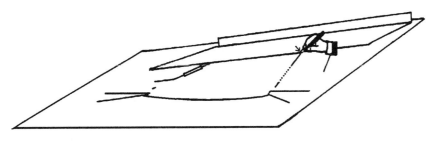

Activity #8 — Illustration 4

STEP #8: Make a second mark on the strip to show the place of the U.L. corner. Next, turn the strip around to the left "wall." Keep the second pencil mark at the U.L. corner. Make a third mark on the manila strip at the D.L. end of the "wall."

STEP #9: Use your right triangular straight edge. Draw perpendicular lines across the manila strip at the three places you have made pencil marks. The straight lines should go over the ¾" part of the manila strip as well as the 2½" part.

Students are evaluated on their teamwork as well as their own efforts.

Activity #8 — Illustration 5

STEP #10: Using scissors, cut along the third line. The smaller section of the strip may be thrown away. The part with the two lines on it will become the walls of your set model.

STEP #11: Turn the folder piece around so that the ¾" strip is closest to you. Using scissors, cut the ¾" strip in the two places you have drawn lines. Cut only ¾". Do not cut the remaining 2½".

STEP #12: Using an X-acto or utility knife, score the 2½" vertical pencil lines. To score means to cut lightly along the line. You do not cut through the manila card completely. You make a gentle cut.

STEP #13: Fold your walls inward. Fold away from the side which you scored (lightly cut).

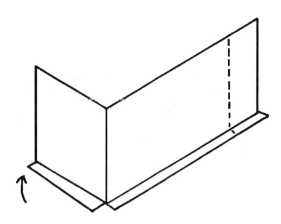

Activity #8 — Illustration 6

STEP #14: Turn the manila walls around so they face you.

(a) Line up the walls along their matching ground plan markings.

(b) Note where doors, archways, windows, fireplaces are located.

(c) Mark their ground plan size at the bottom of your model piece.

(d) Lay the manila strip out flat. Then using your ruler and right triangular straight edge, draw items on the wall. Remember, your scale is ¼″ = 1′. Therefore, a door would be about 1¾″ high and ¾″ wide. Other items should be drawn to scale.

STEP #15: Finish adding practical and decorative detail to the walls. Then tape down the ¾″ flaps on top of the ground plan to hold your set model in place.

You have gained experience drawing ground plans and constructing simple models.

You have completed a study model. You can be proud of your work. Congratulations! You did a first-class job!

UNIT SIX SUMMARY

This chapter has focused on the design of interior sets. They are the most practical kind of set a designer can create for a proscenium stage. You have gained experience drawing ground plans and constructing simple models.

In this unit you have learned:

1. The twenty-six terms used by stage technicians and designers.

2. The eight terms used to describe ground plans and set models.

3. To create three director's ground plans and a mini-model which you built on top of one of your three ground plans.

4. That scenery must fit into a certain space, that actors must be able to move about that space with ease, and all members of an audience must be able to see the actors and the stage.

5. That the designer needs to be precise, accurate and practical.

6. That before designing a set, a designer must read the play several times, talk to the director and find out the kind of set that the director wants created.

Evaluation Guidelines appear on the following page. Your teacher may use this form when determining your grade for the unit.

The designer needs to be precise, accurate and practical.

UNIT SIX EVALUATION GUIDELINES

Student and teammates worked well on Activity #1:   (10) _____

>   Answered a majority of the quiz questions.
>   Raised interesting additional questions.
>   Remained focused on task.
>   Turned work in on time.
>   Teammates participated in follow-up discussion.

Completed first reading of "Box and Cox" on time.   (10) _____

>   Asked questions about plot, characters, setting.
>   Responded to teacher's oral questions.

Completed first "Box and Cox" ground plan with care.   (25) _____

>   Drawings done to scale.
>   Design suggests careful thought about the use of space during the play.
>   Met deadlines and used class time well.

Completed second and third ground plans with care.   (15) _____

>   Drawings done to scale.
>   Designs demonstrate that student looked for alternative solutions.
>   Designs show originality.
>   Met deadlines and used class time well.

With the help of teammates, student completed the mini-model project
with care.   (25) _____

>   The model walls fit around plan well.
>   The decorations on walls suggest the designer's vision of a full-scale set.
>   Student met deadlines and used class time well.

Arrived on time, worked cooperatively in the group, completed work on
time and helped teammates complete their work.   (30) _____

                                                          Total   _____

60-69 = D,   70-79 = C,   80-89 = B,   90-100 = A,   101-115 = A+

NOTE

Theatre is a collaborative learning experience. The greatest number of points are given to students who work cooperatively with their group and who help others.

Getting Acquainted With Makeup

Admit it. You have always been a little curious about makeup. In fact, you may have already experimented with a variety of makeup effects. Most people begin to investigate and play with makeup as youngsters. This interest usually increases around Halloween.

What is your earliest memory of using makeup? Playing with lipstick? Painting lines on your face to make yourself look "old"? Drawing a mustache with black eyeliner? Applying fake scars? Spraying the fake white color onto your hair? Or did you draw red circles on your cheeks, wear a funny wig, and become a clown?

Whatever you did, you enjoyed experimenting with makeup. You loved the effects that makeup created. You became a different person. If you did a good job, even your neighbors didn't know who you were.

Actors use makeup when they perform on-stage for three reasons: (1) to restore natural color and shading that is washed out by bright stage lights, (2) to disguise their natural appearance, and (3) to suggest the age or personality of the character they are playing.

This chapter concentrates on changing your appearance. You are encouraged to experiment with mime, clown and old-age makeup. During this unit, you will become comfortable with the makeup artist's tools and materials. Expect to make mistakes. However, while you are working with makeup, keep the following rules in mind.

Admit it. You have always been a little curious about makeup.

ACTIVITY #1

Learning Sensible Makeup Rules

Purpose of Activity #1

Students will learn the sensible, safety rules for using theatre makeup. These basic rules also apply to personal makeup procedures.

DIRECTIONS

1. Read aloud the following section titled, "Sensible Makeup Rules for Actors." These five guidelines are a safeguard for students.

2. Students apply these rules throughout this unit. In doing so, students will experience greater enjoyment from their makeup experience.

SENSIBLE MAKEUP RULES FOR ACTORS

1. Respect the makeup and the tools. Keep all the items issued to you in your own assigned work area.

2. For your own safety, you will have your own individual makeup kit. Individual kits prevent the spread of infections and disease. Use only your own makeup kit. Do not borrow brushes, sponges, base makeup, rouge, or pencils from another person. Do not share your makeup and brushes with other students no matter how much they beg. It is unsanitary and unsafe.

3. Be creative in using the supplies you have been issued. However, for safety, wait for further instructions from your teacher before experimenting with crepe hair, derma wax, latex, and nose putty.

Taking time to care for your skin will help prevent possible allergic skin reactions.

4. Manage your class time wisely. Allow at least ten minutes of class time to carefully and completely remove makeup from your eyes. It is important to gently remove all makeup from your face. Although most makeups are nonallergenic, take no chances. Remove all traces. Taking time to care for your skin will help prevent possible allergic skin reactions. Carefully follow the directions for removal given by your instructor.

5. Leave time at the end of class to thoroughly clean brushes. Dirty brushes spread disease and infection. Replace lids and caps on all containers. Bacteria and dust in your makeup could cause skin infections. Follow all directions regarding the storage of equipment. For sanitary reasons, leave your work area neat and clean.

ACTIVITY #2

"Beating Up" Your Face With Makeup

On Halloween, trick-or-treaters try to make themselves look "frightening." They paint strange colors on their faces and possibly add a scar or two. This activity encourages you to try to "rough up" your face with makeup. The following instructions explain how to give yourself a black eye, a bruise, a cut or a scar, and a missing tooth.

Purpose of Activity #2

Students will create a black eye, a bruise, a cut or a scar, and a missing tooth. Students will practice the five safety rules from Activity #1.

> *On Halloween, trick-or-treaters try to make themselves look "frightening." They paint strange colors on their faces and possibly add a scar or two.*

DIRECTIONS

1. Use the Basic Makeup Kit that your teacher gives you. It includes an applicator brush, a smooth sponge, a stippling sponge, a brown and a black eyebrow pencil, and several small containers of different lining colors.

2. Bring a washcloth and a small bar of soap for use at cleanup time each day.

3. Use sponges for applying the makeup. The sponge may be cleaned by washing it with soap and water. NOTE: The stippling sponge is made of porous, net-like plastic. It leaves an open pattern of color on your face rather than a smoothly blended, solid patch.

4. Follow the four procedures for creating a black eye, bruises, a scar, cuts, blood, and missing teeth. Enjoy yourself.

PROCEDURE A: CREATING A BLACK EYE

1. For a black eye, actors with lighter skin should choose a blue-gray color. Dab the makeup both above and below one eye.

2. Actors with darker skin may need to select a darker liner. They may also wish to stipple in other colors such as blue, green and maroon.

Activity #2 — Illustration 1

PROCEDURE B: CREATING BRUISES

1. Create a "bruise" on your cheekbone nearest the eye you have already "blackened" with makeup.
2. Experiment with colors other than the ones you used on the eye. The colors should be generally dark. Using the stippling sponge, overlap the "bruised" area with a variety of colors. If you stipple in some red, you can suggest the oozing of blood.
3. Consider adding another bruise on your forehead. Experiment with new combinations of colors and the effects that different types of sponges make.

PROCEDURE C: CREATING A SCAR

Have you ever seen a picture of Frankenstein's monster? He had a great makeup artist.

1. Have you ever seen a picture of Frankenstein's monster? He had a great makeup artist. Today you are the makeup artist. You will create scars on your own face. They can be as big as you wish. You, too, can look like Frankenstein's monster.
2. To make a scar, you will need to use derma wax or nose putty. This is one time your instructor will allow you to experiment with wax and putty. (See Rule 3 at the beginning of this chapter.)
3. Instructions for using derma wax:
   (a) Roll a small piece of the wax in your hand until it has an elongated, worm-like shape.
   (b) Apply the derma wax to the side of your face that does not have the black eye and bruised cheek.

Activity #2 — Illustration 2

(c) Smooth out the edges of the wax cylinder so that it makes a slightly raised bump or "scar." Some sticky wax will remain on your fingers. Wipe it off with a tissue and makeup remover.

(d) Actors may wish to create a reddish-purple scar with makeup. Experiment with new combinations of colors. Making the scar a different color than the actor's normal skin tones makes it more striking. Use a brush to apply and smooth the foundation color.

Actors may wish to create a reddish-purple scar with makeup. Experiment with new combinations of colors.

PROCEDURE D: MORE "DAMAGE": CUTS, BLOOD, AND MISSING TEETH

1. Creating cuts:

   (a) To form a cut on your face, make a little ball of derma wax about the size of a pea.

   (b) Press the wax on your left chin. Smooth it out as you did the scar. You will have just a little bump on the chin.

   (c) Then "pick" at the wax with the wooden tip of a ⅛" brush until you create a tiny "flap." Pull the flap up a little so that it looks like a piece of loose skin. Make sure it is not too loose, or it will fall off. Clean your brush tip immediately after using it.

   (d) Darken the "crater" behind the flap with a gray liner.

   (e) Then with a red liner, draw a trickle of blood coming from the flap of "skin."

   (f) Blood might also drip from a nostril, the corner of your mouth, or one of the bruises.

2. Creating missing teeth:

   (a) This effect is created with a material called black tooth wax.

   (b) First soften the wax in your hand. Then apply a thin layer over one or more teeth.

Cleanup

Allow fifteen to twenty minutes for cleanup. Leave at least ten minutes to thoroughly remove all makeup from your skin. Again, follow directions for removal given by your instructor. Take care not to "scrape" the makeup off your skin. Gentle removal will not create skin irritations.

Leave an additional five to ten minutes to clean your work area. The final cleanup ritual is more important to learn than the various makeup tricks. Without good makeup habits, you can get and spread disease. It is the responsibility of every actor to learn these safety habits.

If you did not have time to try the scar, cuts, or missing teeth techniques, don't worry. You can do them tomorrow. Your instructor has scheduled several days for Activity #2.

Mime Time

Purpose of Activity #3

Each student will sketch a mime mask and then create the mask on his/her face. Students will practice the five safety rules from Activity #1.

[Pantomime artists] are creating an expressionless mask to accompany their wordless performance.

Pantomime artists traditionally cover their faces with a white makeup base. They are creating an expressionless mask to accompany their wordless performance. Often, to reinforce the mask-like effect, they "frame" their makeup at the edges of their faces.

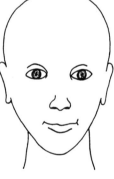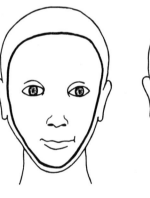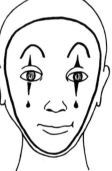

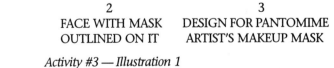

1	2	3
NEUTRAL FACE	FACE WITH MASK OUTLINED ON IT	DESIGN FOR PANTOMIME ARTIST'S MAKEUP MASK

Activity #3 — Illustration 1

For stage performances, most actors blend their makeup into the hairline, under the jaw and over the ears and neck. However, it is difficult and time consuming to remove makeup from the hairline and neck. The purpose of these exercises is to practice creating the mime face effect. Therefore, do all the application activities as "makeup masks" only. You will not blend makeup over ears, neck and jaw.

DIRECTIONS

As you create your mime face, use sketch #3 on page 132 as a guide. You may want to draw that exact design on your own face. Or you may decide to experiment and make changes. Follow the five safety rules from Activity #1.

PROCEDURE A: GETTING STARTED

1. Open your own assigned jar or tin of white makeup base (often called "clown white"). Base or foundation are the words most commonly used to identify the makeup you put on first.

2. Dab some white cream on a clean sponge.

3. Gently spread the cream over your nose. Smooth it out toward the cheeks. Dip the sponge again into your tin of clown white. Spread a thin layer of makeup around your mouth and under your nose. Avoid applying a thick layer.

4. Continue spreading the cream over your entire face covering your mouth, chin, forehead, and (carefully) your eyelids and eyebrows. The eyebrows may need a slightly heavier application. However, with that exception, you want to spread a thin, even layer of white over your entire face.

PROCEDURE B: ADDING DETAIL

1. Once you have spread the white "mask" to your satisfaction, outline your mask with a black eyebrow pencil. The pencil will leave a dark imprint on top of the cream. If you have white makeup beyond the edges of your "mask," wipe it away with a tissue.

2. Draw eyebrows some distance above your normal eyebrows. Draw vertical lines bisecting each eye as shown in the illustration below.

Base or foundation are the words commonly used to identify the makeup you put on first.

Activity #3 — Illustration 2

3. After drawing eyebrows, outline your lips in black.

4. Find the ⅛" brush, and blue eyeliner you have been provided. On each cheek, draw a delicate design of one or more of the following designs: a diamond, a half moon, a star, a daisy, or any other simple shape.

5. If you like the effect, you may wish to experiment with additional designs on the tip of your nose, your forehead, or chin. However, remember that the makeup of most mime artists suggests simplicity.

6. Share your completed mime face with your classmates and instructor. Take a bow. You did a fine job. You also had a good time.

Cleanup

Take adequate time and care. Actors know the importance to their skin of meticulous makeup removal.

Allow twenty minutes for cleanup. Leave ten minutes to gently, carefully and completely clean your face using the makeup remover provided by your teacher. Avoid rubbing off the makeup. Take adequate time and care. Actors know the importance to their skin of meticulous makeup removal.

Again, allow ten minutes to thoroughly clean your brushes, store your clean brushes safely, replace lids and caps and follow directions regarding the storage of all your equipment. These are your materials. Do not share them.

Remember: Taking proper care of your makeup materials is not just a courtesy in theatre. It is a safety necessity! Soiled brushes and open makeup containers can spread infection. Leave your work area cleaner than you found it.

ACTIVITY #4
Research

Purpose of Activity #4
Students will look at makeup books to prepare themselves for creating clown makeup faces.

DIRECTIONS

Activity #4 — Part I requires that you explore a variety of resources with pictures of clown faces including makeup books, children's books, and clown textbooks. You will use these pictures of clowns when you design three clown masks for Activity #4 — Part II.

PROCEDURE

How do you begin researching clowns? Most likely you would try to find pictures of clowns. The two sketches below were drawn from photographs.

Activity #4 — Illustration 1

Do they tell you all you need to know about clowns? Probably not. Before you start designing a clown face, you will need more pictures. Where will you find them?

Research involves asking questions, finding answers, and seeking out facts and pictures. Since childhood, you have been familiar with clowns. However, most likely you have not studied the mouth, nose or eyes of a clown. The clown's facial features are usually exaggerated. The nose and mouth seem to "jump off" the face. Can you answer the following questions?

(a) What are some standard clown mouths that a beginner might copy?

(b) What nose treatments, other than a red ball, have clowns used?

(c) What are some traditional eye designs for clowns?

The clown's facial features are usually exaggerated. The nose and mouth seem to "jump off" the face.

Do you remember the clown white makeup base that you used in Activity #3 — Mime Time? The name of this white makeup base comes from the fact that most clowns wear a white base on their faces. But how many other colors do clowns use in their makeup designs?

Research will help you find the answers to many questions concerning clown traditions. It will also provide ideas for the clown face you want to create for your project. But in what books, magazines or other resources will you find pictures or detailed descriptions of clowns' faces? Are there clown magazines? Are clown makeup books available with color photographs? Or maybe a book about the circus might have pictures of clowns.

Discuss with your teammates nine kinds of books, magazines or special newspapers that might have clown faces or clown makeup. Write your answers in the spaces that follow.

PART I

HERE COME THE CLOWNS RESEARCH FORM

Activity #4 — Illustration 2

_____ _____ _____

_____ _____ _____

_____ _____ _____

Review your list. Then examine a classmate's list. Can you add anything to your list? Next, begin your search. Use the school library, public libraries, your bookshelves at home, children's books, and resources provided by your teacher to locate pictures of clowns.

Clowns have been a source of delight and interest to people for hundreds of years.

Clowns have been a source of delight and interest to people for hundreds of years. Therefore, clown books are popular. There are many clown books and magazines filled with colorful photographs. Find at least four different pictures or sketches of clown faces. Bring them to class.

PART II

Look at the sample sketch on page 137. Sketch three more clown face designs on the neutral plain faces. The plain faces that follow are large enough for you create a realistic design.

- Use a pencil to sketch your clown faces.
- Keep each face simple but different from the other two designs.
- Label colors in each sketch like the sample.

Use your imagination. Like the mime masks, simple designs are often the most effective. Clowns often draw flowers or stars on their cheeks.

Use your imagination. Like the mime masks, simple designs are often the most effective.

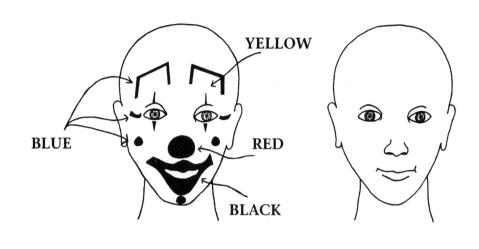

Activity #4 — Illustration 3   *Activity #4— Illustration 4*

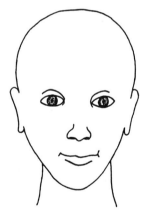   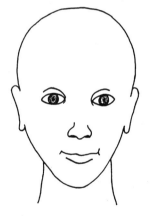

Activity #4 — Illustration 5   *Activity #4 — Illustration 6*

ACTIVITY #5
Circus Time

Purpose of Activity #5

Students make their own faces look like the makeup sketch they have chosen from Activity #4. Students will practice the five safety rules from Activity #1.

D I R E C T I O N S

Select one of the previous sketches as the plan for your makeup design. Before actually applying makeup, you may wish to enlarge the sketch you chose.

PROCEDURE

1. Make your face (or a partner's face) look like one of the sketched clown faces.

2. Use an eyebrow pencil. On your face, lightly sketch the areas of your design that will be filled with a color other than white. The mouth will probably be one area. Other areas may be the tip of your nose and patches around the eyes.

3. NOTE: Your next step will be to apply a base of clown white makeup. Do *not* place the makeup into your hairline. In addition, do *not* cover your neck or your ears. It is difficult to remove clown white from the hair, neck and ears. Your clown face can be a makeup mask. You may decide, however, *not* to put a black border around the outer edges of your mask.

4. Using a sponge, apply a base of clown white except in the areas that you have outlined for another color. Use a lining brush near the areas you have outlined. Spread the makeup so that it forms a thin, even layer.

5. Check your design. Which areas are you going to fill with a red liner color? You have already sketched the spaces for large areas of red on your face. Using a ⅛" brush and red liner color, draw an outline of the large red spaces on your face. Then, with your brush, smooth the red color in toward the center of the space. Your goal is to fill the space with a smooth, thin layer of red color. If the area is large, you may want to use a larger brush for spreading and smoothing the color.

6. Apply one color at a time. When you have finished with the red, clean your brushes thoroughly. Use a little bit of makeup remover and a lot of soap and water. Then repeat the process with a second and third color.

7. Using an eyebrow pencil or black liner and a ⅛" brush, draw the black outline details that you want the audience to see.

8. You may wish to complete your transformation into a clown by finding an appropriate hat and/or a wig.

Use a little bit of makeup remover and a lot of soap and water.

9. Present your completed clown face to classmates and to your instructor.

Cleanup

Allow twenty to thirty minutes to clean up. Clown makeup takes a little more time and effort to remove. Your skin is not used to this makeup and removal process. Do *not* rub off the makeup. You may irritate your skin. Allow ten to fifteen minutes to remove the clown makeup.

After completing Activity #5, you have established safe theatrical makeup habits. Take at least ten minutes to thoroughly clean your brushes, store your brushes safely, replace lids and caps and follow directions regarding the storage of equipment. Leave your work area cleaner than you found it.

ACTIVITY #6

Applying Old-Age Makeup

Many actors try out for school plays. Some are asked to play an older person. In rehearsals these players strive to find ways to make their characters seem older. They may use a stooped posture, a slow, uncertain walk, and props (like a cane or a pipe) to help create the illusion of being old. But most importantly, the actors and the director need makeup to help transform a young person into an older adult.

Old-age makeup covers the face completely. Like mime and clown makeup, old-age makeup completely changes an actor's identify. Old-age makeup allows an actor to portray a character who is completely different from himself or herself.

Old-age makeup allows an actor to portray a character who is completely different from himself or herself.

Purpose of Activity #6

After reviewing makeup books and a video, students learn to create one or more old-age makeup effects on their own faces. Students will practice the five safety rules from Activity #1.

EXERCISE A: VIEWING PICTURES OF OLD-AGE MAKEUP EFFECTS

DIRECTIONS

1. Look at makeup books with pictures of old-age makeup.

2. Using a neutral face template, sketch a design for your old-age makeup. If you do not like your first sketch,

your instructor will give you additional copies of the template on which to draw new sketches.

3. Watch a videotape demonstrating old-age makeup effects.

EXERCISE B: APPLYING OLD-AGE MAKEUP

DIRECTIONS

1. Use the individual stage makeup kit given to you by your instructor for creating special old-age effects.

2. Use one of your sketches as a model to create an old-age makeup effect on your own face.

3. Do *not* share makeup materials with one another.

4. Bring a washcloth and soap to class for removing makeup after this activity.

Do not share makeup materials with one another.

PROCEDURE

1. Make your skin color appear old by applying a base several shades lighter than your normal base. In general, older people have less color in their faces than younger people.

2. To create forehead wrinkles, raise your eyebrows and wrinkle your brow. With a ⅛" liner brush and using a brown or reddish-brown liner, make three very thin lines into the three most visible furrows in your brow. Use a brown liner rather than a black liner and limit the number of "wrinkles" to three. You make a subtle statement about the actor's age. Your makeup looks more natural.

3. To create wrinkles at the corner of your eyes, use your cheek muscle. Squeeze your right eye together at its outside edge. You may see some wrinkles at the corner of your eye. Follow the lines of these wrinkles and create three "crow's feet." Use a brown liner and a ⅛" liner brush. If you do not see any wrinkles, draw in two or three lines where you believe they would appear on an older person.

4. Create sunken eyeballs by using a brown or gray liner and an eyeliner applicator. Lightly cover your right upper eyelid with the liner. Using a sponge, smooth the eye color into the socket of the eye and along the side of the nose. A darker color on the

skin above the eye "sinks" the eye into the skull.

5. Create undereye "bags" by drawing a thin brown or gray line directly below your right eyelid. With the same liner and color draw a "bag" under the eye. A bag represents a sagging of the skin. Later, you will be drawing in a highlight above this first puffy bag.

6. Create deeper "bags" under the eye by drawing a second bag about an inch below the first one using a brown or gray liner. The second bag may be established more with highlighting than with a shadow line.

7. Create "highlights." Highlights accent those parts of the face that stick out and catch light. Highlighting is the use of white or light tan liner. For example, the cheekbones should be lightened. Use a touch of white on each cheekbone and blend it into the base color already on the cheek. A thin white line above each wrinkle line in the forehead should be blended into the brown line described and applied in Step 2. The brown represents the depth of the wrinkle. The white suggests the fold of skin that picks up the light while casting a shadow below. Actors with darker skin may use light tan in places where the above instructions suggest using a brown liner.

8. Create sunken cheeks and jowls. To create a shadow and suggest sunken cheeks, blend a darker color below the second "bag" under each eye toward the ear and the jaw bone. To create cheek jowls, blend a reddish or light gray liner color where you wish to create jowl areas.

9. To create the mouth of an older person, draw a brown line going from the corner of the mouth to the side of the nose. Draw a "highlight" line above the brown line and blend the two lines together.

10. Now look in the mirror. Congratulations! No one will know who you are. Show your special face to your classmates and teacher. If a visitor were to walk into the room, your entire class would look like a group of older adults.

Cleanup

Allow twenty minutes for cleanup. Old-age makeup takes a little more time and effort to remove. Your skin is not used to this makeup and removal process. Do not rub the makeup off. You may irritate your skin. Allow at least ten minutes to remove old-age makeup.

If a visitor were to walk into the room, your entire class would look like a group of older adults.

By now, you have established good actor safety habits regarding makeup. Thoroughly clean your brushes and sponges, replace lids and caps, and follow directions regarding the storage of all of your equipment. Leave your work area cleaner than you found it.

UNIT SEVEN SUMMARY

The makeup safety habits taught in Unit Seven can be applied to your everyday life. Doctors as well as manufacturers endorse these makeup habits.

...the makeup safety habits taught in Unit Seven can be applied to your everyday life.

During Unit Seven you learned many makeup skills.

1. You have been encouraged to experiment with makeup effects.

2. You have learned important safety rules for handling, using and removing makeup.

3. You have discovered ways to change the features of your face.

4. You have learned about the role of research in the planning process of makeup design.

5. You have created special makeup effects such as black eyes, scars and bruises.

6. You have created facial masks which disguise or transform the appearance of your natural features: mime and clown facial masks and age-enhancing character faces.

UNIT SEVEN EVALUATION GUIDELINES

Student showed understanding and respect for rules regarding
makeup use.   (25) _____

> Brought personal cleansing materials to class.
> Did not borrow makeup tools from classmates (or lend them).
> Allowed adequate time for end-of-class cleanup.

Completed Activity #2 successfully.   (10) _____

> Experimented with bruises, scars, cuts.
> Demonstrated an understanding of these makeup techniques.
> Remained on task during class time.

Completed Activity #3 successfully.   (10) _____

> Created mime makeup.
> Remained on task during class time.

Completed Activity #4 successfully.   (10) _____

> Made a list of resources.
> Sketched three clown face designs.

Completed Activity #5 successfully.   (10) _____

> Transformed clown face design from sketch to makeup.
> Remained on task during class time.

Completed Activity #6 successfully.   (10) _____

> Experimented with old-age makeup designs.
> Remained on task during class time.

Arrived on time, worked cooperatively in the group, completed
each activity and helped teammates complete their work and
succeed.   (40) _____

                                                    Total _____

60-69 = D,   70-79 = C,   80-89 = B,   90-100 = A,   101-115 = A+

NOTE

Theatre is a collaborative learning experience. The greatest number of points are
given to students who work cooperatively with their group and who help others.

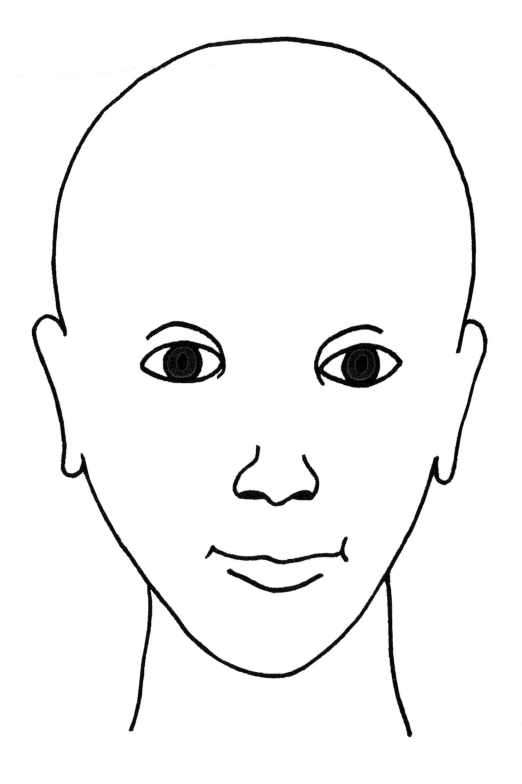

Illustration: Full Face Template

Theatre Business

Unit Eight discusses the practical side of the Theatre Cube, BUSINESS. At times, actors may think that they are the most important members of the theatre team. But as we have learned throughout this textbook, theatre is a collaborative experience. Everyone plays an important role in theatre and contributes to the success of a project.

Unit Eight places the spotlight on one of the most important groups of people in the theatre: your audience. Without an audience, actors do not have a purpose for performing. Without an audience, theatre artists cannot earn a living.

> *Without an audience, actors do not have a purpose for performing.*

The business staff brings that audience to the theatre. They create an attractive theatre-going experience. The business staff is responsible for making the audience want to return to the theatre to see future plays.

Many repertory theatre groups require everyone in the company — actors included — to perform a business or technical job. Other groups require that all actors rotate jobs as an apprentice to specialists in lighting, set design, business, makeup, costumes and props.

The following individuals provide service to your audience: the poster makers, ticket sellers, program designers, advertising salespersons and ushers.

ACTIVITY #1

Learning About the Theatre Business Staff

Purpose of Activity #1

After reading and discussing the information in Activity #1, students will better understand the importance of theatre business.

DIRECTIONS

1. Read aloud the following sample project.

2. Discuss ways in which you think the drama club could raise money for the trip.

A SAMPLE THEATRE PROJECT:
HOW TO RAISE $600 FOR A DRAMA CLUB TRIP

Imagine that the drama club at your school has decided to raise some extra money. Members want to attend a nearby theatre festival and the club needs to clear $600 for the trip. In the past, students have been able to raise $200 with bake sales, a car wash and similar promotions. You have to raise an additional $400.

This time the club decides to present a play. As members of the drama club, you consider the size of your "theatre" and the number of people who have attended past performances. You decide that you can expect to sell $400 worth of tickets.

But that will not be enough money. The club needs to spend money in order to produce the play. You may have to rent costumes, buy lumber for sets, and pay for certain props and other items. You must purchase scripts and pay a royalty fee as well.

You need to raise an additional $200 dollars for production costs. Possible solutions to your problems are to sell more tickets, reduce production costs, and sell advertising space in your program.

Ushers and ticket takers are not always listed in a play program. And they never take a bow at the end of a performance.

Theatre business does not get much attention in high school theatre classes. Ushers and ticket takers are not always listed in a play program. And they never take a bow at the end of a performance.

But remember the Theatre Cube described in Unit One. The following individuals are equal partners in the enterprise we call theatre: the students who plan the programs, the students who create and put up the posters, the students who sell the tickets and advertising, and the students who make certain that bills can be paid. They are the unsung heroes in the high school drama program. Often, they are under-appreciated in professional theatre companies as well.

ACTIVITY #2

Planning a Fundraiser

Purpose of Activity #2

Students will learn to budget costs for a play production. By participating in Activity #2, you will learn to plan a fundraiser.

DIRECTIONS

1. Your instructor will divide the class into teams of four to six members. Each team will have a similar cast of characters. Each group will deal with the same problems and requirements. The setting for this role-playing activity is a high school. You will be portraying students at the high school who are also members of the drama club.

2. Your team will role-play Activity #2. Each committee member estimates his/her costs in this activity. Your team is trying to achieve a balanced budget.

3. Everyone in your group reads the section titled, "The Problem" which describes the committee's financial concerns.

4. Read aloud the following procedure. This section describes the six members on the committee and the problems they are trying to resolve.

5. Everyone on your team will choose one of the committee members to role-play. If there are only four team members, the students who choose to be Members 5 and 6 will play two roles.

6. Member 6, the business manager, is the team organizer.

THE PROBLEM

Your team has to raise $600 total to take a theatre trip. Some members have pledged to raise $200 through bake sales, a car wash, intermission refreshment sales, and contributions. You still need to raise $400.

The club has decided to present the play "Box and Cox" as the fundraiser. Your team hopes to make $400 in ticket sales and $200 in advertising. However, each committee member has his or her own budget needs.

Your team can only spend $200 or less on production costs.

Your team hopes to make $400 in ticket sales and $200 in advertising. However, each committee member has his or her own budget needs.

PROCEDURE

Activity #2 is a budget meeting.

1. Read the descriptions of each of the six committee members.

2. Read the sample budget. Your team will create its own realistic budget. Members of the team will submit realistic requests for money. Everyone's goal is to complete each job so that you can have a successful production. All drama club members want to satisfy the audience as well as the performers and workers behind the scenes. The team understands that it must make $400 after expenses for the trip.

3. After you complete Activity #2, Member 5, the director, will explain to the class how his/her team worked cooperatively to agree on their budget. The explanation may be a summary delivered by Member 5, or it may be a dramatization performed by all team members.

4. Play your roles. Stay in character. Try to get your fair share of the budget. Remember: Some compromises will be necessary in order to help the business manager keep costs at or under $200.

5. In Activity #2 you will estimate your costs. For Activity #3, "Calculating Your Budget," you are expected to have more precise cost figures.

Member 1

1. You are the **scene designer.** You are responsible for constructing the sets. In order to create a set, you will need lumber and muslin to make flats. Your set design will need a fireplace, a window and two or three doors. You must also paint the scenery once it is built.

2. Calculate the amount of money you will need. Prepare a list of expenses for the business manager.

Member 2

1. You are **head technician** in charge of lights, sound and properties. The director wants to use nineteenth-century music in the background at appropriate places during the performance. You need to buy a blank tape on which to record the music. You may have to purchase a tape or disk containing that music. Or use music from the public library.

2. A major prop needed in "Box and Cox" is a canopy bed. You will need to build one. Therefore, you need to budget money for lumber and paint. Will other props cost money as well? Consider creative money-saving alternatives.

3. From the $200 total production budget, estimate how much

money you will need. Prepare a list of expenses for the business manager. Think of creative ways to economize.

Member 3

1. You are the **costume designer**. "Box and Cox" takes place in the 1850s. It has only three characters. However, you want their costumes to show that these people are living in a different century. Will you make the costumes? Will it be cheaper to rent them? How much will it cost to make them? To rent them? Consider creative ideas to save money.

2. Do not forget that Cox is a hatter. He tries on several hats before leaving in the morning. Where will you locate appropriate nineteenth-century top hats?

3. Calculate the amount of money you will need. Prepare a list of costume budget expenses for the business manager.

Member 4

1. You are the **assistant business manager** in charge of posters, ticket sales and programs. Your posters must be attractive enough to bring an audience to the theatre.

2. The drama club expects you to raise $400 in ticket sales and $200 in advertising. How many people can occupy your theatre? How many people can you realistically expect to see "Box and Cox"? What amount will you charge per ticket?

3. In addition, Member 4 designs and estimates the cost of programs. What information will it include? How many pages will you need? Plan to provide at least two additional pages for the display of ads. Advertising generates income. How much will it cost to print the program and the tickets?

4. From the $200 total production budget, estimate the amount of money you will need. Prepare a list of expenses for the business manager. Find someone to donate materials or services.

5. When your team begins Activity #3, "Calculating Your Budget," you, the assistant business manager, will be in charge. Review Activity #4, "Recording Your Specific Prices." Consider how you want to organize your team.

Member 5

1. You are the **director.** You are also your team's spokesperson, responsible for reporting to the entire class. You tell the class the decisions that your team made and how you arrived at

You [the director] tell the class the decisions that your team made and how you arrived at these decisions.

these decisions. If your team decides to "act out" your report, then you get to play "director" in real life. You will actually direct other members of your team in an improvised report.

2. As director of "Box and Cox," you should accept the following facts:

   (a) You chose to direct "Box and Cox" because you like the play. It is funny. You consider it a challenge to get a high school audience to see its humor.

   (b) Only three actors volunteered their time for this fundraiser. In your opinion, they are perfect for the roles of Box, Cox and Bouncer.

> *The faculty has always been understanding and supportive of drama activities at the school.*

3. You have only one budgetary consideration: complimentary tickets. The faculty has always been understanding and supportive of drama activities at the school. In return, the drama club has offered them complimentary tickets as a way of saying "thank you." You want to continue this practice.

4. Member 5 wants to set aside twenty tickets for this purpose. However, that means that the assistant business manager will have to revise ticket sales estimates. They will not be quite as high as $400. Therefore, the complimentary ticket costs will come out of the business manager's $400 budget.

5. Member 5 will make a list of the students' names and the roles they are playing. Make two copies of this sheet. Give one to your teacher at the end of the class period. Give the other list to Member 6.

Member 6

1. You are the **business manager**. Therefore, you are the leader in charge of this role-playing exercise. Your job is to organize the members of your team. You must persuade your team to divide the budgeted $200 production money fairly. Remind your group: They are also allowed to spend less than $200 and to come in under budget!

2. A sample budget is displayed on the following page. Create your own team budget that is similar to the sample. The one you make should also have a statement of expected income. However, your estimated budget sheet will show team members' estimated expenses. Your final budget will reflect information provided by team members from their Activity #4 figures. Remember: Everyone on the team has to agree

upon the expense budget.

3. Today, everyone's figures are approximate. The anticipated expenses will probably exceed $200. You must consider how they will trim the budget. Give your teacher a copy of your unbalanced budget at the end of the first day.

SAMPLE BUDGET FOR THE FUNDRAISING ACTIVITY

Income		"Box and Cox" Expenses	
Ticket sales for "Box and Cox"	$400.00	Lumber and hardware	$ 58.00
		Paint supplies	$ 16.00
Advertising in the program	$200.00	Lights and sound	$ 14.00
Bake sale	$60.00	Properties	$ 10.00
Car wash	$80.00	Costume rental and/or materials	$ 52.00
Intermission food sales	$40.00	Poster materials	$ 8.00
Contributions	$20.00	Printing costs for tickets and program	$ 20.00
TOTAL	$800.00	Makeup	$ 18.00
		Complimentary tickets	$ 14.00
		Royalty fee	-0-
		TOTAL	$200.00

NET PROFIT: $600.00

ACTIVITY #3

Calculating Your Budget

Purpose of Activity #3

Your purpose is to accurately research true prices for items you need in your budget. By contacting hardware, lumber, costume and secondhand stores, you will learn more about theatre business.

By contacting hardware, lumber, costume and second-hand stores, you will learn more about theatre business.

You are still playing your committee member role from Activity #2.

1. Reread the sample budget. The figures on the right side neatly add up to $200. However, they are not totally realistic. They do not express the needs of the students on your team. Your homework assignment is to find accurate prices for the items you need.

2. Phone or visit local hardware and lumber stores, costume shops, printers, and other merchants. Get cost estimates of the items for which your "character" is responsible.

3. Make budget calculations regarding the cost of materials and rentals based on your phone calls or visits to stores.

4. Speak with teachers and other personnel around school. They may suggest ways in which you can cut costs or they may have materials that you can borrow. Here is the partial list of people you might consult: technical theatre supervisor; librarian (for appropriate music, recording equipment); music department technicians; industrial arts teacher; art teacher; home economics teacher; building custodians; and the print shop supervisor.

5. Seek out neighbors or relatives who may have props, old-fashioned clothing, or hats which you could borrow. Does a classmate own a canopy bed or an old-fashioned hat rack? Maybe you remember seeing a costume or hat on display in a store window or in a secondhand clothing store. Would the merchant allow you to borrow an item in exchange for a credit line in the program?

6. Use your imagination freely. Who can help you? Does a local church have clothes for rummage sales? Can you look at some of them? Does the church have tables you can borrow?

Make budget calculations regarding the cost of materials and rentals based on your phone calls or visits to stores.

ACTIVITY #4

Recording Your Specific Prices

Purpose of Activity #4

Each student records the specific prices from his/her research and more clearly understands theatre business.

DIRECTIONS

You are still playing your committee member role from Activity #2. Write the following information on a piece of paper. Your instructor will collect Activity #4, "Recording Your Specific Prices."

1. List the stores you called. List the prices that they quoted for certain items. Also list any items that stores were willing to loan you in return for putting their name in the program as free advertisement. List any free services offered by small neighborhood stores, other schools, or churches. Ask and you will receive.

2. List the neighbors, relatives and friends that you called. List any items you can borrow, and any free services offered by parents, sisters and brothers, relatives, neighbors, church members, or teachers.

ACTIVITY #5

Designing a Play Program

The theatre business staff is responsible for designing and printing the "playbill" or program. Programs give audience members background information about a play and list the names of cast and crew members. They can also be an important source of revenue.

Purpose of Activity #5

Your group's purpose is to design and produce an actual play program. By participating in Activity #5, you will learn more about theatre business.

Programs give audience members background information about a play and list the names of cast and crew members.

DIRECTIONS

You are still playing your committee member role from Activity #2. Your group is responsible for creating a mockup copy of the program for "Box and Cox."

1. Member 4 from Activity #2 will guide the team. He/she will assign one page of the playbill to each teammate. Everyone is responsible for developing his/her page in detail. Your completed program design will be displayed for other teams to examine.

2. With the help of team members, Member 4 will decide how many pages the program will have and how many pages will be used for advertising.

3. The rest of the group will suggest other information that might appear on the remaining pages.

4. Essential facts that must be included are: (a) the play's title, the author's name, and name of the publishing company; (b) information about where and when the story takes place; (c) a list of characters and the actors playing each role; (d) a production crew list; and (e) acknowledgments.

5. For additional program details, ask yourself if all six sides of the Theatre Cube are represented in the program.

6. You may want to include two additional items in your program: a request for contributions to your fund-raising cause and the title and date of the next drama club production.

7. If you have too much copy for the space available, Member 4 will decide what items need to be cut from the program.

ACTIVITY #6

Creating an Actual Play Program Page

Purpose of Activity #6

Your purpose is to design and produce an actual page for a play program. When you complete Activity #6, you will understand the challenges of theatre business.

DIRECTIONS

1. Lay out or paste up the "Box and Cox" program page for which you are responsible.

2. Your teammates will decide on the size of the program pages. Use that size paper for your individual mockup.

3. Carefully measure each piece of information for your page.

4. Precisely place all items on the paper. You may rule margins, draw and write copy by hand. Or you may choose to use a computer.

5. Do the best job you can. Your teacher will consider neatness and clarity when evaluating your contribution to the team effort.

6. Place your name, date and class period on the back of the page. Come to class prepared to combine your pages of the program with those of your teammates.

UNIT EIGHT SUMMARY

This brief unit discussed the practical side of the Theatre Cube — BUSINESS. The poster makers, ticket sellers, program designers, advertising salespersons and ushers provide service to one of the most important groups of people in the theatre — your audience.

In Unit Eight you have learned:

1. That everyone involved in a production performs an invaluable role.

2. About the business responsibilities of set designers, light technicians, costume designers, poster makers, ticket sellers, program designers, advertising salespersons and ushers.

3. To raise money for a drama club project.

4. To determine specific costs for your own budget area.

5. To design a play program.

6. To create an actual play program page.

7. To understand and respect the importance of theatre business.

You have learned that everyone involved in a production performs an invaluable role.

UNIT EIGHT EVALUATION GUIDELINES

In each unit in this course, you will be a member of a team. Your team will work collaboratively to make certain that everyone finishes his/her work and succeeds. The evaluation guidelines at the end of every unit will give maximum points to a student's contributions to the team.

MEETING DEADLINES

1. Completed Activity #3 and Activity #4 on time.   (20) _____
   Arrived in class with a list of inexpensive sources.
   Arrived in class with a revised budget request.

2. Completed Activity #6 on time.   (20) _____
   Appropriate page size and content.
   Layout is neatly and carefully arranged.

COLLABORATIVE TEAM EFFORT

3. Participated fully in team activities, cooperated with everyone   (40) _____
   on team, made good use of class time and took pride in doing
   quality work.

4. Accepted offers of help from team members, worked hard, and   (35) _____
   helped others on team.

                                                        Total _____

70-79 = C,   80-89 = B,   90-100 = A,   101-115 = A+

NOTE

Theatre is a collaborative learning experience. The greatest number of points are given to students who work cooperatively with their group and who help others.

Semester Project
On-Stage and Off-Stage Roles: Fitting the Pieces Together

Theatre is a performing art. People in theatre have a goal. That goal is to communicate feelings and ideas to their audience. Therefore, it is natural for a theatre class to combine its talents and present a final performance.

This final project is similar to a chorus or orchestra concert. You have a chance to practice the skills you have learned this semester. You will also provide enjoyment to family, friends, students, and other members of your community.

This final project is similar to a chorus or orchestra concert. You have a chance to practice the skills you have learned this semester.

This unit will discuss: working cooperatively both on-stage and off-stage, choosing an audience, choosing performance dates, choosing a play — one-act, scene, storytelling, or puppet play — to perform, and accepting responsibilities.

The subtitle of the *Theatre Arts 2 Student Handbook* is "On-Stage and Off-Stage Roles: Fitting the Pieces Together." Students fit those pieces together in Unit Nine. *The Theatre Arts 2 Student Handbook* emphasizes collaborative learning in theatre and each unit stresses the need for theatre artists to share their talents and work as a team.

A drama class should end the semester or year with the creation of theatre. Creating theatre involves the cooperation of many artists. Unit Nine gives you the opportunity to share your talents. For the final performance, each student will fulfill an acting and two non-acting roles. Each person is dependent on every other member of the team. When everyone works cooperatively, the entire team is successful.

ACTIVITY #1

Choosing a Performance Date

Purpose of Activity #1

With the help of their instructor, students will choose a performance date.

DIRECTIONS

1. Read aloud paragraphs A, B, C and D.

2. Choose a performance date now for your semester performance. Often it is difficult to secure a date that meets the needs of the principal, the students and the audience. Therefore, you need to choose a performance date several months before your semester performance.

A. Early in the semester the class and the instructor need to choose a performance date. Finding a good time to perform at the end of the term is often difficult. Select a date and stick to it.

B. You have a responsibility to the total group to perform your roles as an actor and as a technical worker on that final performance day. When a person is absent on the performance day, he/she undermines the team's efforts. In order to be successful the performance depends upon all students and the teacher to do their assigned jobs.

C. Everyone works together as one large group in Unit Nine. It is your entire group's responsibility to be ready for your semester performance. Theatre is a shared experience. Everyone needs to work together to produce a successful production. No one person is more important than another person in theatre. Stagehands, costume designers, makeup coordinators, and lighting technicians are as important to the production as the actors.

You are important to the group. Do not forget that.

D. You are important to the group. Do not forget that. This final performance is a test of real "collaborative" theatre. The group works as a single body. This is a "no excuses" performance. The group's cooperation has a greater influence on an audience than any one person's performance.

ACTIVITY #2

Choosing an Audience

Purpose of Activity #2

Students will participate with the teacher in the selection of an audience for their semester performance.

DIRECTIONS

1. Read aloud paragraphs A, B and C.

2. Discuss the advantages and difficulties of performing off-campus for an audience, such as one junior high school class. Discuss the advantages of performing on-campus in the evening for family, friends, fellow students and neighbors.

A. Since theatre is a collaborative effort, students will participate with the teacher in the selection of an appropriate audience for the end-of-semester project. In most instances, that audience will be parents, relatives, friends and fellow students. A day performance would be convenient for fellow students. A night performance might be best for parents, relatives, friends and neighbors. Therefore, your class might consider giving two performances, one during the school day and another in the evening.

B. If possible, you may want to "travel" with your performance. That is, you could take your production outside your school. Several audiences might enjoy seeing your performance such as a children's ward at a hospital, a grade school class, a church group, or a group of older adults.

C. You will need to answer the following questions if you perform off-campus. In what area will you perform? Do you need props, lights and scenery? Can you move scenery, props and lights there easily? Will actors need to be excused from classes? How will they get to and from the performance site?

A day performance would be convenient for fellow students. A night performance might be best for parents, relatives, friends and neighbors.

ACTIVITY #3

Time, Talent and Money: Thinking About the Semester Project

Purpose of Activity #3

Everyone will examine the three necessary elements for presenting a final performance and will better understand the procedure for planning a semester project.

DIRECTIONS

1. Read the following sections titled, "Time," "Talent," and "Money."

2. Discuss the section dealing with Time. You already have the Talent in the class.

3. Discuss the section on Money. You do not need a great deal of money to present a showcase production — a puppet show, a storytelling festival, or an evening of monologs. These shows often require minimal sets, lighting, sound or costumes.

TIME

A. Your class needs at least four weeks to complete most semester projects. Some will require more time.

When you fail to meet deadlines, or if you fail to have deadlines at all, everyone suffers.

B. Setting deadlines to accomplish various tasks is essential. When you fail to meet deadlines, or if you fail to have deadlines at all, everyone suffers.

C. All workers must create a personal calendar for each day of the project from Day One to the final cleanup day following the performance. The calendar will describe the sequence of tasks to be accomplished and deadlines to be met.

D. Make certain that you allot a reasonable amount of time to accomplish your project. Do you have a month remaining in which to complete the project? Do you have only a few short weeks? Adjust the type of performance you choose to the number of weeks you have to rehearse.

TALENT

A. Everyone in this class is hard-working and talented. You have already demonstrated those traits in each of the past units. Now, as a team, you have to decide what type of performance you wish to give.

B. Everyone in the class will be assigned two roles to perform — an acting role and a non-acting role. If most people in your class have displayed an interest in monolog performances, storytelling, or playwriting and performing, your instructor may choose a project which calls for many actors. If other students reveal a strong interest in design, your teacher may find ways to make use of those important talents also.

MONEY

Most semester projects do not require extra funds. Discuss the following questions if you choose a project that requires spending money.

- How much money is available to support an elaborate project?

- Will your school be able to provide the materials you need to carry out your project?

- Can scripts be purchased, or will you choose one of the student-written scripts from the playwriting unit?

- Will your school allow you to duplicate original plays on its copier?

- Do you need lumber or other set building materials?

- Does your school have a "costume closet"? Can students in your class use the costumes?

- Are funds available for the rental of costumes or other equipment?

ACTIVITY #4

Choosing the Best Performance Option to Meet the Needs of Your Class

What is the most difficult decision that you and your instructor will make? It will be choosing the play, scene, or short story that you will perform. You will have to consider many factors such as the amount of time you have before the scheduled performance date, the audience(s) you will be performing for, and the class's commitment to the project. Three different types of performances are described in Activity #4. They are listed in the order of difficulty — the easiest to the most difficult.

What is the most difficult decision that you and your instructor will make? It will be choosing the play, scene, or short story that you will perform.

Purpose of Activity #4

Students, with the help of their instructor, will choose the best semester performance option to meet their needs.

DIRECTIONS

1. Read aloud the following section titled, "Three Performance Options."

2. Discuss the advantages for Option 1. List them on the board. Are there any disadvantages? List them on the board.

3. Discuss the advantages for Option 2. List them on the board. Are there any disadvantages? List them on the board.

4. Discuss the advantages for Option 3. List them on the board. Are there any disadvantages? List them on the board.

THREE PERFORMANCE OPTIONS

Performance Option #1

The Showcase performance. Short on time? Is the group not quite ready to produce a short play or one-act? The Showcase performance is the least demanding of the three types of final project.

A. In this type of production, members of your class can "showcase" the work they have created in the previous *Theatre Arts 2* units. You may wish to perform your own scenes or short plays from the playwriting and puppetry units. Other students may wish to perform a monolog or present a storytelling.

B. This Showcase type of presentation requires careful planning and organization. You will need rehearsal time for the individual selections and the coordination of the various "acts" into a smooth flowing hour of entertainment. The Showcase performance is popular with audiences.

Performance Option #2

Finding new materials to perform. The second type of presentation also involves a collection of different theatre pieces. Class members choose new pieces to study, rehearse, and perform. This second option is more difficult because additional memorization and rehearsal time is required.

A. Everyone will need time to search out and locate appropriate scenes to do. Moreover, you may have problems sharing rehearsal space. However, most students enjoy the excitement and challenge of doing new scenes. You have an opportunity to develop new characterizations and to solve new problems.

B. The scenes you select may involve more than two characters. However, avoid scenes with more than four characters in them. Larger casts make self-blocking more difficult. Some class members may feel that doing new scene work is too risky. They should choose scenes from the playwriting and puppetry units or monolog and storytelling presentations.

Performance Option #3

Presenting a one-act play by the entire class. This third type of performance involves the entire class in the presentation of a complete one-act play. Casting, coordinating, and

> **A drama class should end the semester or year with the creation of theatre.**

rehearsing the one-act requires about three weeks of class time. This option is attractive because everybody in the class works together.

A. **Problem 1:** Most one-act plays do not have large casts. Often *many* students enroll in theatre classes. Finding a play with roles for every actor will be difficult.

Solution 1: You could divide the class into two groups, then you would rehearse and perform two separate one-act plays. Each one-act should have a moderate-sized cast. Everyone in class deserves an acting role. This goal is more important than keeping the class together in one group.

B. **Problem 2:** Two plays require two separate rehearsals at the same time. This situation could add confusion to the schedule. You also would need to construct two different sets for the two plays.

Solution 2: Choose a one-act with a cast of seven to ten characters. Plan to present the play two or three times. Each time, use different actors in the roles. This is called double or triple casting. Sometimes, certain shorter roles are played by the same actor in all performances while other players switch off. Naturally, double casting requires that you give more than one performance to more than one audience.

It takes time and energy to get a one-act play ready for an audience. The class must be ready to make a serious commitment if it chooses this option. On the other hand, the benefits are great. It is thrilling to begin with a play script and end up with a polished performance of a complete play.

It is thrilling to begin with a play script and end up with a polished performance of a complete play.

ACTIVITY #5

Reading Activity:
Being a Member of a Larger Team

Purpose of Activity #5

After reading aloud Activity #5, students will better understand the collaborative nature of theatre and the meaning of "teamwork."

DIRECTIONS

1. What does the word "teamwork" mean to you? List the meanings of the word on the board.

2. Read aloud the following section titled, "Teamwork Means..."

3. Then read aloud and discuss the section, "How Would You Feel?"

Teamwork is as important in theatre as it is on the playing field.

TEAMWORK MEANS...

Teamwork is as important in theatre as it is on the playing field. Do not let your team down by missing rehearsals, neglecting a job you have agreed to do, or being absent for the final performance.

A. Teamwork means memorizing lines on schedule. When you fail to meet deadlines, you slow everyone else up.

B. Teamwork means working with rehearsal props and costumes.

C. Teamwork means contributing extra time and energy to the project.

D. Teamwork means helping the class locate, build or create props, scenery, or costumes for the entire group.

E. Teamwork means helping the group with a non-acting job like painting, posters, or prompting.

F. Teamwork means encouraging others. It means offering help and friendship to those who need it.

HOW WOULD YOU FEEL?

1. How would you feel if your teacher decided not to show up for your final performance? Would you be angry? Would you feel that he/she let you all down?

2. Suppose your teacher was responsible for all of the costumes for the final performance. It was his/her job to locate proper clothing for all cast members. How would you feel if your instructor decided not to come to the performance? Suppose he decided he did not feel well; or his parents wanted to take him out to dinner for his birthday; or he was tired and just did not want to go to your performance that particular evening.

3. Several of you are probably saying, "A teacher can't do that!" or "He/she wouldn't do that!" Why couldn't a teacher do that? Why wouldn't a teacher do that to his/her class?

4. Discuss how you would feel if several actors were absent on the day or night of the final performance? Suppose they were per-

forming in your play or puppet show. You were depending on them. Would you be disappointed? Perhaps you had worked hard to direct the play. You knew that it was necessary for all performers to be present if the play were to be successful. Would you be angry if they were not present to say their lines? Would you feel that your teammates let you down?

5. Discuss how your teacher would feel if several actors were absent on the day or night of the final performance? Do you think that the teacher would be disappointed? The teacher has worked hard to ensure that everyone experiences success. If you were the teacher, what would you say to the team members waiting to perform? Explain your thoughts.

ACTIVITY #6

Production Responsibilities:
Working Collaboratively as Part of a Larger Team

Purpose of Activity #6

Students read a list of backstage job descriptions to determine which two jobs they might like to perform.

DIRECTIONS

1. Read aloud paragraphs A, B and C. Reminder: Your teacher will assign every student both an acting and two non-acting roles to perform.

2. Read aloud the backstage production roles necessary for a successful play. Select four jobs that you think you would like to perform.

A. When a professional theatre company presents a play, it hires dozens of non-acting company members who contribute to the final product. We say these people work "backstage" or "behind the scenes." Some do technical work with scenery, lighting and costumes. Other people provide coaching and training for actors. Still others tend to the business and audience needs of the theatre.

B. In amateur and high school theatre, fewer people are available to do backstage work. Therefore, many actors work behind the scenes in addition to performing in scenes. Your instructor's primary objective during the semester project will be to involve everyone as actors. However, everyone in

When a professional theatre company presents a play, it hires dozens of non-acting company members who contribute to the final product.

class will have a non-acting responsibility as well. The acting responsibility fulfills a course objective. The non-acting responsibility helps to meet a group need.

C. It is hard to predict what your group's behind-the-scenes needs will be. They will depend on the material you choose to perform. After reading your list of preferences from Activity #7, your teacher will assign you two behind-the-scenes roles.

It is hard to predict what your group's behind-the-scenes needs will be.

BACKSTAGE JOBS

Playwright: Author of an original scene or one-act play.

Director: Responsible for blocking and guiding actors in a scene.

Assistant Director: Assists teacher/director; maintains prompt script.

Producer: Coordinates all segments of the project; monitors deadlines.

Safety Director: Assists producer; focuses on reducing safety hazards.

Set Designer/Builder: Responsible for building and placement of scenery.

Designer's Assistant: Helps the set designer with the building and placement of scenery.

Electrical Technician: Responsible for lights, sound and special effects.

Property Coordinator: Locates, organizes and keeps track of props.

Graphic/Scenic Artist: Assists others needing drawing/painting skills.

Costume Coordinator: Locates, sews and takes care of costumes.

Makeup Coordinator: Supervises design, purchase and care of makeup.

Business Manager: Oversees budget, transportation, expenses and ushers.

Assistant Business Manager: Responsible for programs, posters and publicity.

Stage Manager: Oversees all backstage operations during performances.

ACTIVITY #7

Production Responsibilities: Stating Your Preferred Production Roles

Purpose of Activity #7

You will list the four roles that you feel you could perform with enthusiasm. From this list, your instructor will assign you two backstage jobs to perform in addition to your acting role.

DIRECTIONS

1. Select four role descriptions from the list of backstage jobs described in Activity #6.

2. Place your name on a blank sheet of paper.

3. List your four choices. Your teacher will assign you two of your job choices.

ACTIVITY #8

Making a Personal Production Calendar

Purpose of Activity #8

You will learn to create a personal calendar. This personal calendar will set deadlines and define daily goals for accomplishing specific tasks.

This personal calendar will set deadlines and define daily goals for accomplishing specific tasks.

DIRECTIONS

1. Place your name on a blank sheet of paper. Then write your first backstage role "title" for the final class project.

2. Skip four lines. Write the tasks you will have completed by the day of the final performance. Then indicate the jobs you will perform to accomplish these tasks.

3. Fill in the four empty lines described in #2 above. Indicate the jobs that you need to complete for the final performance. Also indicate cleanup responsibilities.

4. Write your second role "title." Make a list of jobs similar to the ones you created for your first role.

5. Create a personal calendar which describes your daily classroom activities from now until the post-performance cleanup. Simply state your primary and secondary role objectives on your calendar. Make two copies of this calendar.

   A. Include early, middle and late deadlines: For example, "ground plan completed" or "lines memorized" or "costume fitted."

   B. Include conferences with the teacher, director or other coordinators.

   C. Include deadlines set by coordinators.

   D. Include dates or deadlines for the purchase of supplies.

A sample student calendar follows. Follow this format when you create your own calendar, or develop your own format for your production calendar.

...your instructor will assign you two backstage jobs to perform in addition to your acting role.

PRODUCTION CALENDAR

Monday	Tuesday	Wednesday	Thursday	Friday
1 1ST REHEARSAL Read through play.	**2** Block opening scene. (After school) Meet with director to discuss props.	**3** NO REHEARSAL Work on lines from opening scene. Make props list. Find an assistant.	**4** Block second scene. Decide what props need to be built. Make building plans with assistant.	**5** Block final scene. Post prop list. Ask class for possible sources for locating props.
8 NO REHEARSAL Begin building needed props. Schedule future prop gathering activities.	**9** Do opening scene with lines memorized. (Evening) Make phone calls seeking lenders of props.	**10** NO REHEARSAL Work on lines. More building of props.	**11** Rehearse second and third scenes. If a school truck is needed to pick up any props, schedule these pick-ups.	**12** Rehearsal: scenes to be announced. Work on lines. Find and clean up area for safe storage of props.
15 REHEARSAL: Scenes to be announced. Plan makeup design. (Evening) Arrange for pick-up of props.	**16** REHEARSAL DEADLINE FOR ALL LINES TO BE MEMORIZED. (Evening) Pick up props.	**17** Run through first half of play with props. (After school) Meet with director. Any new needs? Any problems?	**18** Run through second half of play with props. Design prop table layout.	**19** Costume parade. Run through part of play. Set up prop table. Store props after rehearsal.
22 (In class) Experiment with makeup. (Evening) Dress Rehearsal	**23** Polish scenes that need work. (Evening) Dress rehearsal	**24** PERFORMANCE at assembly (10:00) Set up props in advance. Store props after performance.	**25** Help strike set and clean up backstage. Return props to fellow actors.	**26** Phone: Thank patrons for lending props. (After school) Return props.

Name: Sarah Bernhardt   **Primary role:** Mrs. Bouncer

Class: 7th period   **Secondary role:** Properties

Activity #8 — Illustration 1
Sample Student Production Calendar

At the beginning of Unit Nine you read that theatre is a performing art. Throughout this text as well as this unit we have learned that a performer does not function alone. He or she must depend on the contributions of many valuable backstage team members.

In your semester project you have several important roles to play. You are an actor and a backstage worker providing valuable behind-the-scenes support to other actors. In this unit, you are contributing a unique and special service to a larger team — your classmates.

UNIT NINE SUMMARY

While working on this final project, you applied many of the skills introduced in other chapters. More importantly, you experienced the challenge of taking a script and turning it into a theatrical performance that entertains and enriches the lives of an invited audience.

In Unit Nine you learned:

1. To follow other classmates as well as lead them.

2. To select appropriate material for the group to perform.

3. To set a production date and then accept it.

4. To select an audience.

5. To provide behind-the-scenes assistance.

6. To work cooperatively as a group in order to produce a final showcase or one-act play.

7. To give a final performance.

8. That no one on a team is more important than anyone else. Everyone serves an important role in theatre.

9. The true meaning of Teamwork.

In Unit Nine you utilized and reinforced many skills that you already knew.

1. You planned and met deadlines.

2. You found appropriate costumes.

3. You solved problems creatively and cooperatively.

4. You memorized lines.

5. You interpreted a script.

6. You developed a character.

In Unit Nine you utilized and reinforced many skills that you already knew.

...a few of you will have explored new roles in theatre...

In addition, a few of you will have explored new roles in theatre:

- Producer
- Director
- Lighting Technician
- Resident Playwright
- Stage Manager
- Business Manager

UNIT NINE EVALUATION GUIDELINES

MEETING DEADLINES

1. Memorized lines on time for acting role.   (20) _____

2. Located appropriate costume for role.   (10) _____

3. Arrived in class on time with appropriate materials.   (10) _____

4. Made certain that the play, storytelling, monolog, or puppet   (25) _____
   play in which the student participated was ready for the
   final performance date.

COLLABORATIVE TEAM EFFORT

5. Arrived on time, participated fully in production jobs, took pride   (30) _____
   in doing quality work and made good use of each class session.

6. Provided support and help to other students and contributed to a   (20) _____
   superior team effort.

                                                                    Total _____

70-79 = C,   80-89 = B,   90-100 = A,   101-115 = A+

NOTE

Theatre is a collaborative learning experience. The greatest number of points are given to students who work cooperatively with their group and who help others.

Since class members will also be serving as actors in the semester project, your teacher may use the Theater Class Performance Evaluation form to assess student performances. Below is a copy of this form.

Theatre Class
Performance Evaluation

Name _____

Project _____

	EXCELLENT (4)	GOOD (3)	FAIR (2)	POOR (1)	NONE (0)
MEMORIZATION, PREPARATION					
MOVEMENT, BLOCKING					
CONCENTRATION					
ARTICULATION, DICTION					
PROJECTION					
EXPRESSION, CHARACTERIZATION					
RATE OF SPEECH					
POISE, STAGE PRESENCE, APPEARANCE					
ENERGY, CREATIVITY					
OVERALL EFFECT					
READY ON TIME					
Subtotals					
Total					

Unit Nine - Semester Project
173

STUDENT PRODUCTION CALENDAR FOR SEMESTER PROJECT

PRODUCTION CALENDAR

Monday	Tuesday	Wednesday	Thursday	Friday

Name: _____

Class: _____

Primary role: _____

Secondary role: _____

Five Short Essays

Theatre Ethics, Etiquette, Safety, History and Superstition

When was the last time you heard the word etiquette? Maybe your mother used that word in church. "Act right! Use proper etiquette!" Or perhaps your grandmother said, "Where are your manners? That's not proper etiquette!" Have you also heard someone use the word "ethics"? Maybe you heard a neighbor or an actor or a newscaster use that word. "Dorthea is a very ethical person." "That congressman is unethical!" Unethical, as you know, means not honest or fair.

The words etiquette and ethics share more than just the same first letter of the alphabet. Both words have a common concern: courtesy and the consideration of others. They both stress "doing the right thing." Unit Ten does not require you to participate in activities in order to learn ideas. Rather, Unit Ten asks you to think. Often student textbooks do not raise the topic of ethics. We think that it is important for our future intelligent adults to think about and discuss a variety of topics.

This unit offers five short essays on theatre ethics, etiquette, safety, history and theatre superstitions. Enjoy Unit Ten.

THEATRE ETHICS

Ethics is the stronger of the two words, ethics and etiquette. A person who is being unethical is not just being discourteous. He is breaking a law or requirement. In theatre, copyright laws are the ones most frequently broken.

The word copyright means that the author or the publisher owns the rights to the actual words written in a play, story, poem or text. These words have been registered with the Library of Congress. The words are then protected by law. If a play or book is protected by copyright, no one can "borrow" or steal those words to put into another book or play. Furthermore, people cannot legally photocopy or duplicate pages, chapters or entire copyrighted works.

Photocopying pages of books, plays and magazines is

A person who is being unethical is not just being discourteous. He is breaking a law or requirement.

Photocopying pages of books, plays and magazines is common today. Furthermore, copying pages is easy and convenient.

common today. Furthermore, copying pages is easy and convenient. People photocopy all types of written items at the supermarket, the post office, photocopying stores, schools, offices and even their own homes.

But just because it is easy to photocopy pages does not mean it is always legal or "right" to do it. You might say, "Well, everyone does it. And besides, no one will ever find out if I photocopy someone else's book or song or work." An answer to these statements might be: Just because everyone does something, does not make it moral or ethical. Do not be certain that no one will ever know. After a recent lawsuit against major photocopying centers, companies make it their business to obey copyright laws.

Why do we have these copyright laws? These laws were created to protect the writer and publisher. People write and publish for a living. Just as a store owner sells goods for a living, writers sell their books, plays, or songs for money. Writing is their daily job and if people illegally photocopy their materials, writers cannot earn a living.

Most plays written and published in the last 100 years are protected by copyright laws. What does that mean to you? Let's say that your school is planning a performance of a copyrighted play like *Our Town*. Publishers require that schools, community theatre groups, or professional acting companies buy scripts from them. To make photocopies of entire scripts or even scenes is illegal and unethical. It denies the playwright and the publisher the opportunity to make a living from a creative work of art which they own. Furthermore, it is against the law.

In addition, publishers may charge a royalty for public performances of a copyrighted play. Most of the plays performed at schools are royalty plays. What does that mean? It means that the school must pay the publisher a set amount of money for each performance given. The publisher then forwards a contract percentage of the royalties to the author of the play. Professional play companies are charged a higher royalty rate than amateur groups.

Sometimes teachers photocopy a script for a play that they wish their students to perform before an audience. It is against the law for anyone to make and distribute copies of any copyrighted scripts. If a person wants to photocopy a script, the person must call the publisher and ask permission.

You are probably saying, again, "That's a lot of trouble. And besides, everyone photocopies everything these days." Just because everyone does something that is against the law, does not make it right. Someday, the person breaking the law will be caught. People who break copyright laws are caught and prosecuted.

Some schools feel that they cannot raise enough money to pay royalty fees. These schools can appeal to publishers for special consideration. Or they can choose non-royalty plays to perform. However, if schools produce royalty plays and just ignore or refuse to pay the fees, they are being unethical and they are breaking the law.

Under copyright laws, the playwright owns the dialog written for a play. It is illegal to make cuts or change "offensive" words without getting written permission from the publisher and/or author. It is best to contact the publisher in writing before making any changes to a script that you are planning for public performance.

It is illegal to make cuts or change "offensive" words without getting written permission from the publisher and/or author.

Note that these laws apply only to public performances. If a monolog is performed in the classroom, your teacher should have the right to decide what language will and will not be used in that setting. It is not a public performance.

However, when shows are presented on your auditorium stage, your teacher, director, or principal may face a problem. If the play has questionable language, your principal may want to make small changes. But he/she needs to know that, for public performances, no one can make changes in a script unless he/she gets permission from the publisher. The principal or director can call the publisher. The publisher might say it is all right to make these changes. Or the publisher may say that no changes are allowed. In that case, the teacher will have to choose another play without questionable language.

Do most directors do this? Probably not. Are those teachers who do not get permission being unethical? That is a question that might be a good topic for classroom discussion. If one word in a script is offensive and the director replaces it with an appropriate but milder word, must he write a note to the publisher? What about three such words or phrases? Ten? Who should decide at what point actions that are well intentioned and practical become unethical?

In addition, creative artists in music receive a royalty.

Every time you buy a recording, a portion of your purchase is a royalty fee for the recording artists and the composers of the songs. Similarly, each time a song is played on the radio, a composer receives a royalty.

Therefore, if a camp group or a school make photocopies of a song or music for a public play or camp jamboree without paying a royalty, they are breaking the law. Many people will tell you, "Why, everyone copies songs all the time. And besides, no one will ever know that I am doing it." If someone breaks the law, that person is breaking the law. Period! To make photocopies of sheet music or the words of a song is illegal and unethical. It denies the writer of the musical work and the publisher the opportunity to make a living on a creative work of art which they own.

In addition, most school districts provide a budget for classroom textbooks. But sometimes teachers do not know that there is money allocated for texts. In those cases, a teacher may buy one textbook and photocopy that book to give to each of his/her students. School districts do not know that they are doing this. Your school district would prefer that teachers buy each student a textbook rather than break the law.

School districts know that it is against the law to photocopy a textbook without the permission of the publisher. Your school district understands that it is an author's job to write a textbook. Authors support their families from their jobs. If teachers photocopy their books, the writers will not be able to make a living. They will stop writing textbooks.

Before you can make responsible choices, you need to be aware of other people's rights.

Few theatre textbooks in the past have mentioned the topics of copyrights, royalties, ethics and legality. One reason may be that it is a subject that students have little control over. But some of you will be tomorrow's theatre actors and teachers. All of you will be bright, thinking adults. Moreover, each one of you is now making moral and ethical decisions everyday. You face ethical dilemmas in your life. Before you can make responsible choices, you need to be aware of other people's rights. You need to choose to do the right thing.

ETIQUETTE

Backstage Etiquette

Mention the word etiquette to a theatre person and that person will probably think about appropriate behavior for audience members. Audience etiquette is important. However, this essay will discuss rules of etiquette among people back-stage and on-stage.

Shakespeare wrote, "All the world's a stage and all the men and women merely players." We can also turn that statement around. "All stages are miniature worlds and all the players merely men and women." What does that mean? It means that all people are created equal. All people have equal rights and responsibilities. Therefore, all theatre people, stage-hands, technicians and actors are equal.

Sometimes actors become over-impressed with their own importance. Lead performers may begin to view themselves as royalty. They feel that they deserve more privileges than other actors or technicians. Bit players may wish to assert their importance by being rude to stagehands. Watch out! This kind of thinking and behavior leads to bad feelings, friction and disaster.

Backstage etiquette means that everybody is working together to make the production successful. Each person has an important role to play. Each person must respect the needs and dignity of other members of the company. Try patting the backs of your fellow workers. Recognize their contributions to the show. That type of behavior will insure a show's success.

Try patting the backs of your fellow workers. Recognize their contributions to the show. That type of behavior will insure a show's success.

If anyone is to be considered "special," it should be the stage manager. He or she is responsible for seeing that all players are in their places and working together. The stage manager's job not only takes skill, it often takes a miracle.

On-stage, actors usually observe some additional rules of etiquette regarding their fellow players. When a character is speaking, the author expects the person who is speaking to be the center of attention. Other on-stage actors can help focus audience attention by looking at the speaker.

Nonspeaking actors can also avoid unnecessary or unchar-acteristic movements. Movements across a stage make a viewer think, "What's going to happen? Why is he doing that?" Therefore, do not move while someone else is speaking unless a director tells you to move.

Stage etiquette suggests that actors move while delivering their own lines. They may also move when their character is intended to be the person in strongest focus. Stage dialog is like a game of catch. Each time you speak, you are throwing the "ball" to another player. You want him to catch it and become the center of attention. When he speaks, he has the attention. However, while that person is speaking, he is looking for another receiver. You remain still and focused knowing that you may be that receiver.

Audience Etiquette

You are entering a theatre. At that moment, there are certain appropriate behaviors that the actors expect of you. Actors are entitled to possession of the stage during a performance. During a play, it would be rude if audience members got out of their seats, walked down to the apron, walked up a short flight of steps and strolled across the stage to a convenient exit on the other side!

It would be just as discourteous for an audience member to rise from his seat and announce in a normal voice, "I'm going to get a drink of water!" And then go up the aisle, and exit through the lobby door.

...some folks often fail to use common sense and common courtesy. They need to learn about theatre audience etiquette.

Most actors have "war stories" to tell about rude audiences they have observed. Normally, people who go to a play do not mean to be rude. However, some folks often fail to use common sense and common courtesy. They need to learn about theatre audience etiquette.

In any theatre audience, there are usually some viewers who have never been to a play. This statement is probably more true today than it was years ago. During the 1940s and early 1950s people went to see plays almost as often as movies. Many people did not even own a TV. Today, television and movies influence our lives. Today many people do not think about going to see a live performance.

When viewers do go to the theatre for the first time, they have already watched many movies. They have probably spent years in front of a television set. Sitting in a theatre, people often think, "This is just like going to the movies." Or, "This is just like watching TV." But it isn't!

The actors on a screen cannot hear an audience member cough, munch on popcorn or talk to the person sitting next to him. Moreover, the movie actors cannot see someone get out of his seat and inch his way past other viewers during a tense moment.

Movie actors cannot hear or see the audience. They

cannot feel your presence. Screen actors cannot get excited by a sudden hush in the crowd as one of the characters slips a knife from a table drawer. Nor can they predict how long to wait when a single sob in the audience causes a chain of other quiet reactions.

On the other hand, live performers can see, hear and feel your presence in the audience. An electricity flows between a theatre audience and the performers. Laughter, applause and emotional reactions all communicate important messages to the actors. They are messages of encouragement. These actors can hear. Even silences speak loud and clear! When actors know they are communicating to their audience, they offer even greater performances.

An electricity flows between a theatre audience and the performers. Laughter, applause and emotional reactions all communicate important messages to the actors.

Unfortunately, the coughs, popcorn munching and talk also send a message. "Sorry, Mr. and Ms. Performer, but we are concerned with our own lives. We cannot give you our full attention."

If you were an actor on-stage, how would that kind of implied message affect your performance? Granted, it is not always possible to silence a cough. Also, an occasional whispered message to a neighbor like "What did she say?" does not mean that you are being grossly discourteous. It is the constant talking and questioning that irritates actors and audience alike.

The rules of audience etiquette are more demanding when the performance is live. Show your reactions with appropriate applause, sighs, laughter or gasps. But do not show off. The people on-stage are the characters the audience came to view. If your behavior makes people look at you, you are stealing the scene and showing disrespect. If your throat gets dry and you cannot stop coughing, quietly go to the lobby. When you feel better, return to watch the play.

While we have you in the lobby, let's talk about getting to the theatre on time. On time means getting to the theatre before the lights dim and the curtain rises. In most plays, the first spoken lines reveal important information.

People who get to their seats promptly deserve the right to listen without interruption. It is unfair to have latecomers climbing over their knees and blocking their vision. In addition, some plays begin with a highly charged scene. Sometimes a single actor is on-stage. Other times, the entire company sings an opening number.

Some companies announce at the beginning of a show that they will not seat anyone until after the first scene.

Performers also have a right to be heard. They have a right not to be interrupted by people looking for their aisle and seat numbers. Some companies announce at the beginning of a show that they will not seat anyone until after the first scene. If you find that you must wait to be seated, do not become angry. Just try to be on time for plays in the future.

Play performances often have intermissions. These provide you with an appropriate time to use the restrooms. They also give you an opportunity to ask questions or express opinions about the play you are watching.

Sometimes food and beverages are on sale in the theatre lobby. Usually, patrons are not allowed to take these items back to their seats. This rule curbs unnecessary noise and avoids unwanted spills. Try to finish your food and drink during the break. A bell, an announcement, or a buzzer often signals the end of an intermission.

It is common courtesy to return to your seat before the curtain rises on the next act. In short, theatre etiquette expects that you plan when you get up and return to your seat. You are considerate so that you will not disturb other viewers or the performers.

Sometimes theatre and English classes go to see live play performances on field trips. The performances may be special matinees. These afternoon plays are arranged to serve viewers from many schools. Some actors love to perform to student audiences. Many actors enjoy students because they react openly to action on-stage. The electricity between performers and audience is strong and the energy level is high.

On the other hand, a few veteran actors have called these matinee field trips "Creature Features." And the creatures they have in mind are the students. These actors point to several roadblocks that make it difficult to get and keep the audience's attention.

First of all, many viewers are attending a play for the first time. They are unaware of proper theatre etiquette. Moreover, they are there because they have to be or they feel it is a good way to get out of classes for half a day. They have no true interest in seeing the play.

Secondly, many of these students will sit among a group of friends. Their loyalty to their friends is stronger than their commitment to the actors on-stage. Let's look at an example.

Maria is seated three seats away from Robert. She makes an inappropriate comment. Robert is more likely to laugh at Maria than to pay attention to the actors on-stage. At a regular evening performance, Maria would be less likely to talk loudly. If she did, she would probably get disapproving looks from people sitting nearby.

Next, consider the friends at the matinee who are not close by. They may be from another school and seated halfway across the theatre. For many students, entering the theatre is like going to an assembly. You want to be seen and to see others. A good deal of calling out and waving takes place before things settle down. Even after they do, it may take a while for the actors to break through the bonds already made by members of the audience. The actors then need to establish themselves and the play as the center of focus.

The veteran actors say that occasionally, teachers do not help the communication process. Some teachers do not want to go on field trips. They may either act like a tyrant or act as if they have the day off.

Teachers can make the experience more valuable by briefing students about proper theatre etiquette. They can discuss appropriate behavior while watching a play. Teachers may also supply the students with some background informa- tion about the play. Viewers may have an easier time understanding a difficult play if they have read and discussed it before attending a performance.

As a reader of this essay, you, too, can contribute to the success of your theatre experience. Bring to the theatre your own memories as an actor. Remember the bond you felt when you performed before friends, family and strangers. One of the great miracles of theatre is that both viewers and actors are participants. Try to give the players your full attention.

If other members of the audience are rude or disruptive, ignore them. They probably have had little or no experience watching a live performance. If the opportunity arises, try to educate nearby offenders. Use tact. Set an example with your own behavior. While on a field trip, if people show a lack of theatre etiquette, write a letter to the editor of your school newspaper. Describe what you believe is proper behavior.

This essay has centered around issues that are alive today. These issues will still be important in the future. As theatre stu-

Viewers may have an easier time understanding a difficult play if they have read and discussed it before attending a performance.

dents, you will probably become tomorrow's theatregoers. Several of you will become the directors, producers, actors and other theatre artists of the twenty-first century. Together, the theatregoers and the theatre makers will preserve what is good about theatre. Ethics in theatre management and appropriate theatre etiquette are a part of what is good in theatre.

SAFETY

Theatre safety is a necessity. It is *not* an option such as, "Should we do it safely or should we do it easily?" You must decide to choose safety for your sake and for the sake of your fellow students.

Too often actors, directors, stagehands and crew members leave safety to chance. Everyone is concerned about one thing only: getting the show ready on time. Therefore, many actors and crew members willingly take shortcuts. They overlook possible hazards that they are creating.

In haste, people leave lumber and tools on the work room floor. Anyone can trip over these items and injure themselves. Or, an off-stage escape stairway has no guardrail because the carpenter is still finishing the on-stage banister that the audience will see. A director says, "Forget bracing that platform; we need a window shade for tonight's rehearsal." A wardrobe assistant leaves a hot iron unattended while helping an actress pin up her hem.

We cannot allow safety to take a back seat to careless, dangerous practices.

Everyone defends his/her own actions. Theatre members say, "I had no choice. We were in a hurry." "I left everything in a mess because it was a necessity." A necessity? Theatre safety is a necessity. We cannot allow deadlines to control our good sense. We cannot allow safety to take a back seat to careless, dangerous practices.

Often students, directors, technical crew, and even teachers begin to think: "Nothing is going to happen to me. Accidents may happen to someone else. But not me." Or, "Theatre students should be able to make a few changes and improvise to save time." Or, "Two of us can handle that rope without a counterweight." An overconfident attitude encourages us to take foolish risks.

What can a theatre class or company do to become more aware of safe practices? How can theatre students and professionals learn good habits? They can take two steps: appoint a safety director, and schedule safety orientation meetings at the beginning of every production run or at the start of every semester.

In theatre, a good director or producer tries to find the best people for each job. The director looks for the most qualified, reliable actors, set designers, costume designers and lighting technicians. Therefore, it makes good sense to fill the role of safety director with the most competent person for that job.

...it makes good sense to fill the role of safety director with the most competent person for that job.

The Job of Safety Director

The safety director's responsibilities include: reading about common dangers in theatres, finding which problems exist in this particular theatre, suggesting new ways of changing old habits, and purchasing equipment that will reduce the risk of accidents or injuries.

For example, a safety director may read that it is a health risk to share makeup. Then she would recommend that the theatre department buy lining brushes in bulk. The makeup supervisor or troupe advisor would then issue one brush to each performer in a play. Replacement brushes would be available for everyone to purchase at the school bookstore.

In addition, personal makeup kits would be on sale at the bookstore. By buying in bulk and selling at cost, schools would make the kits more affordable. If all chorus members in a show are to use the same color lipstick, the safety director might recommend slicing up a single lipstick. Chorus members would then receive pieces of lipstick on butter pat trays.

The safety director would also be responsible for making a pre-performance check. Often, "last minute" safety measures are forgotten because of deadline pressures. She must supervise the completion of certain safety chores: posting a "low clearance" sign; placing luminescent tape on stair treads; properly storing spray cans and other hazardous solvents; taping down electric cable running along the stage floor; and repairing an exit light.

However, the safety director's most important job is to schedule a series of meetings with cast and crew members of a play production. Beginning with the first production meeting, the safety director would assist crew chiefs. She would describe standard safety procedures for handling materials and tools that could cause injuries.

Every single person associated with the theatre should be told about the location and use of the first-aid kit and fire extinguishers. These meetings would help everyone understand how to respond to an emergency. Moreover, they would serve as a reminder that "this theatre group takes safety seriously."

Safety Precautions for Backstage Crews

Using Power Tools Safely

Work crews use many tools ranging from a needle to a table saw. The most dangerous tools are power tools. Accidents occur when a person using a power tool is either careless or overconfident. When using power tools, most people know that they should wear safety goggles to protect their eyes from flying particles. But all too often, they do not remember to put them on. Or worse, technicians remember to use the goggles but do not choose to wear them. They are in a rush and think, "Nothing is going to happen to me."

Sometimes backstage newcomers are embarrassed to admit that they have never used a particular tool before. They say to themselves, "It is not that difficult. Besides, I have watched other people use it." Then they charge ahead, tacking, cutting, drilling or gluing. This course of action can lead to injury.

Every backstage worker should receive some instruction on the proper use and storage of tools. Ladders should be one of those "tools." There are proper ways to carry them and proper ladders for different jobs. Workers should be alerted that a simple hand tool, like a utility knife, can injure someone seriously. Circular saws and other dangerous power tools should be locked up. They are to be operated only by an instructor or under his or her personal supervision.

Using Lighting Equipment Safely

Light boards control a great deal of amperage and volts. Spotlights give off intense heat. Therefore, backstage workers must be carefully trained before they install or use any lighting equipment. Safety note: When focusing lighting instruments, use heat resistant gloves.

Most lighting instruments are hung above the stage or above the audience. Therefore, technicians must use ladders or catwalks to get to the pipe where they want to mount or adjust an instrument. This is not a serious problem, as long as the workers use sturdy wooden ladders, caution and good sense.

One of the major causes of electrical accidents in theatres is an overconfident "I-know-how-to-do-it" attitude. Faulty wiring can be a major fire and safety hazard. Most wiring problems can be traced to plugs and connectors which have been hastily attached to the ends of electrical cables. Technicians must check and double check new wiring before plugging it in. Take your time. You will save lives.

Using Paint, Solvents and Chemicals Safely

Toxic vapors, solvents and caustic chemicals are another source of possible danger in technical crew work areas. One of the best safety measures is to select products, like paint, that contain few or no harmful chemicals. Another safety precaution is to be sure that work areas have adequate ventilation or fresh air when crews are using spray cans or glues. Safety note: Backstage workers should be warned that several plastics, including Styrofoam, give off deadly gasses when heated.

Backstage workers should be warned that several plastics, including Styrofoam, give off deadly gasses when heated.

Operating the Fly System Safely

Some high school theatre buildings have a space that stretches twenty to twenty-five feet above the stage floor. That space is called the fly loft. It is used as an area in which to hang scenery and curtains out of the audience's view.

During a performance this scenery may be dropped behind or in front of other scenery that has been built on-stage. The arrangement of cables, pulleys, counter-weights and other hardware is called the fly system. "Flying" scenery "in," onto the stage, or "out," back up into the loft, permits a stage crew to make scene changes in a matter of seconds. However, fly systems also can be a source of danger.

In theatres with a fly system, heavy pieces of scenery are suspended over the heads of the actors. This scenery must be carefully and securely tied to the pipes that support them. There is always the possibility of a freak accident with the fly system. Safety note: Stagehands must be certain that no one is on-stage when the scenery is lowered.

Does your school have a fly system? Do you work backstage? If so, your teacher will tell you exactly how it works. Furthermore, he will introduce you to additional terms like batten, grid, arbor and rigging. You will learn the precautions that everyone should take in order to operate the system safely. Safety note: Do not work on a fly system until you have received careful training from the supervising teacher.

Your present school theatre may not have a fly loft. However, in the future, you may work in a theatre that has a fly system. Do not be afraid to admit that you do not know how to operate the equipment. Ask someone to "show you the ropes." Remember: Do *not* work on a fly system until you have received careful training from the stage manager. Other people's lives depend on you.

Dangers Actors Face and Safety Precautions

When meeting with actors the safety director needs to discuss six areas of safety concern: hazards concerning nails, flats and lighting behind the set, stage combat, makeup, scene changes and special effects, horsing around and the post performance strike.

Nails, Flats, Lighting and Actors

Actors find protruding nails on a set more by touch than by sight. If they are lucky, it will be their costume that gets snagged and not their skin. Safety note: Actors should report these nails. They should then check to see that these problems are solved. Poorly lit passageways or a stage brace beside an exit are also potential hazards. They make movement behind the scenes dangerous. Safety note: Changing actors' backstage traffic patterns and providing extra practice time may solve some of the problems.

Stage Fighting and Actors

The only people who should touch stage weapons are the people who have been trained by a knowledgeable adult.

Any type of staged fight can cause injuries. Slaps and struggles must be carefully choreographed by a trained fight director. When guns or swords are involved, even more care must be taken. Safety note: Actors should not play with weapons laid out on a prop table. The only people who should touch stage weapons are the people who have been trained by a knowledgeable adult. Remember: these are real weapons. They can cause serious harm if precautions are not taken.

Makeup and Actors

Most theatrical makeup has been manufactured so it may be applied and removed with comfort and ease. However, some makeup is more complex. Prosthetics, bald caps, and hair pieces call for adhesives and solvents that must be used with care. Most actors are aware of these problems and are properly cautious. However, many actors do not seem to be aware of the danger of infection that comes from sharing makeup materials.

For many years, schools and amateur theatre companies provided a central supply of makeup. Everyone in the cast used this same supply. Some actors used their fingertips; some used sponges, and others used brushes. Most of the applicators — especially the fingertips — were dirty. They already had been dipped into other makeup creams or liners. Much of the makeup was carelessly left out on shelves, uncapped and not cared for. Eventually, it was put away, ready to be hauled out and used again several weeks later by dozens of different actors. These actors' fingers and brushes would add to the collection of bacteria and oils deposited on the makeup. Safety note: Is this the situation at your school today? If so, decide now to work for a change in makeup use and habits. Group makeup kits are a breeding ground for bacteria and disease. They spread infection. All actors should own their own makeup kits. In the interest of health and safety, you should demand your own makeup kit.

All actors should own their own makeup kits. In the interest of health and safety, you should demand your own makeup kit.

Scene Changes and Actors

During the run of a show, stagehands lay out props, move scenery and provide appropriate light and sound cues. In certain multiple set productions they must make major scene changes between acts. In musicals, the scene shifts are even more frequent and complex. Safety note: Actors should make every effort to keep out of the way of stagehands. Your safety is threatened if you are in the wrong place when scene changes are made. Furthermore, when people block the stagehands, it can add precious seconds to the length of the scene change.

Special Effects and Actors

Are you curious about magic acts? Do you want to know how an "explosion" works on-stage? Actors need to curb their curiosity about special effects that technicians set up just before or during a show. Safety note: Flashpots used for explosion and smoke effects are particularly dangerous. If you feel you must know more about them, let an expert demonstrate their use in a well-lighted, carefully controlled place. Backstage, before a performance, is not the right time to play with fire.

Practical Jokes and Actors

At times, students become bored waiting for their next cue. They play practical jokes on one another or signal to players on-stage. Performance and rehearsal sessions are not a good time for "horsing around." Your actions distract others. Moreover, they could cause injury. Remember: you are "playing" in a work area. The stage is semi-dark and full of objects that can hurt someone. Pushing and playing tricks can lead to injury. Even if you are performing in a comedy, take your job seriously. Be a professional.

Striking the Set

Frequently, actors are asked to participate in a post-performance strike. "Strike" means to take apart the walls, platforms and stairs of the stage set. It also involves the proper storage of flats, lighting equipment, sound cables, props and costumes. When a strike is over, the stage is bare. Sometimes, "strike" is scheduled right after the final curtain, before the cast party begins. Technical directors who choose to strike at this time can cite good reasons for doing so.

Unfortunately, "safety" is not one of them. Everyone is in a rush to dismantle the set quickly. They are looking forward to the party. Under these circumstances, actors fail to see bolts and nails jutting out of flats and lumber. Others, who are unfamiliar with proper storage procedures, leave equipment where it can be damaged or can be a hazard to passersby. With too many people on-stage trying to "help," someone usually ends up with a few bumps and bruises. Occasionally, an injury can be more serious.

It does not matter whether the strike is on Saturday night or the following Monday. Actors should try to avoid adding to the chaos and confusion. Safety note: Find one job that you understand and do that job with care.

At another meeting, actors can be advised about the hazards in handling firearms, curtains, trap doors, props and even furniture.

The moral of this essay is: Avoid careless behavior. Take the time to care — for yourself and your fellow theatre members. Take care by showing concern for safety — yours and everyone else's. Remember the cautions described in this essay. If you do, "Break a leg!" will continue to be a theatre expression meaning "Good Luck" rather than a grim reminder of the accidents that can occur.

HISTORY

Theatre Arts 2 has examined ways in which a variety of talented artists interact and support one another. Working together, they produce "theatre." At the beginning of this book you created a model in the shape of a cube. Arrows on the cube suggested the interdependence of theatre craftsmen.

Two sides of the cube have not been discussed in this text. This essay briefly introduces theatre history. However, the text does not delve into the subject in detail. Moreover, *Theatre Arts 2* does not include a chapter on directing. Why?

The *Theatre Arts I Student Handbook* devotes a unit to the director's craft. Therefore, the topic of directing was not included in the *Theatre Arts 2 Student Handbook*. Students who are interested in directing can obtain a copy of *Theatre Arts I*. Then ask your instructor to let you pursue an independent directing project.

If you were to explore directing in depth, you might seek out books by directors of great distinction like Konstantin Stanislavski and Peter Brook. You might also find information about past productions of the play you have chosen to direct. Or read about the author and other plays he's written. You would do this because you need to know some history in order to perform your job effectively.

Theatre history is important. As you continue your study of theatre, you will need to know about the origins of theatre crafts in a variety of cultures. You should also become familiar with the great writers, actors and thinkers of the past. We learn a great deal from books and from people who know the traditions of theatre.

As you continue your study of theatre, you will need to know about the origins of theatre crafts in a variety of cultures.

However, this book has emphasized participation in theatre activities. Each chapter had an end product.

1. You constructed a cube.
2. You told a story.
3. You wrote dialog.
4. You performed a monolog.
5. You designed and created a ground plan.
6. You designed facial masks with makeup.
7. You produced a budget and playbill program.

The study of theatre history is a more passive activity. You read or you listen. And, possibly, you prepare for a written test. The authors of this text decided that a formal study of theatre history should be postponed and introduced in a more advanced class.

Students can participate in a theatre history activity by preparing an extra credit report. Students can work in teams to create the report. Sharing the work with team members is more enjoyable than doing a report alone.

Choose one small aspect of theatre to investigate. Choose a topic of particular interest to you and your team members. Make a colorful and lively presentation to the rest of the class. Limit your oral report to five minutes. Following are several topics for you to consider.

1. Black playwrights of the twentieth century
2. Commedia dell'arte and its influence on modern theatre
3. How the Globe Theatre helped shape Shakespeare's plays
4. Kabuki Theatre traditions
5. Peking Opera
6. A biography of any important theatre personality
7. A portrait of a legendary theatre company

    The Moscow Art Theatre

    The Abbey Theatre

    The Federal Theatre
8. The growth of musical theatre in the United States
9. Theatres of ancient Greece

SUPERSTITION

Superstitions are fascinating. People get "hooked" on certain old sayings and keep them alive.

Every culture has its own peculiar superstitions. Many subcultures or groups also share beliefs that have grown out of old wives' tales rather than fact. Superstitions are fascinating. People get "hooked" on certain old sayings and keep them alive. "Don't walk under a ladder." "If the palm of your hand itches, you will receive money or good luck soon." "Don't let a sweeping broom touch your feet. It will bring bad luck." Theatre people have their own superstitions too.

Did you know that many actors consider it bad luck to utter the name Macbeth in a theatre? If you forget and do mention his name in conversation, you must turn around twice to ward off the evil consequences. Actors will tell you that productions of *Macbeth* have often been struck with troubles: fires, accidents, even death. Therefore, actors honor the superstitions as a way to avoid bad luck.

Did you know that it is also bad luck to say "Good luck" to an actor who is about to open in a play? Instead, theatre people say "Break a leg!" In addition, you may have heard that players and stagehands never whistle backstage. It is bad luck.

Of course not all theatre superstitions predict doom and disaster. Rain on opening night is said to be a good sign. Actors believe in many other good signs. Like athletes, sailors, circus performers, truck drivers and medicine men, some performers wear or carry personal good luck items.

Other performers follow certain good luck rituals. They feel these behaviors will insure that the play will be a success. Some acting companies form a circle, join hands and spend a moment in silent communion before a production. On Broadway there is said to be a "Gypsy robe." Dancers in musicals are called "Gypsies." These dancers pass the Gypsy robe from company to company on opening nights. It is welcomed as a symbol of support, encouragement and success.

Some acting companies form a circle, join hands and spend a moment in silent communion before a production.

Have you ever heard the expression: "A bad dress rehearsal means a good opening night." This phrase must have been invented by a frustrated director. She may have been trying to find something encouraging to tell her cast after a disastrous final rehearsal.

Almost every experienced theatre artist can tell you about a horrible dress rehearsal. They will insist that company members forgot their lines, missed entrances, overlooked light cues and ripped their costumes. The tech crew worked with jammed doorknobs and falling scenery. "And the following night, it was a miracle! Everything went perfectly." Don't you believe it.

• Things probably did not go smoothly on opening night.

• If they did work smoothly, then everyone sacrificed a great deal of time at the last minute. They worked together as a team. It was hard work that made the performance a success, *not* a miracle.

Most disastrous dress rehearsals do not have a perfect ending. A lot of adrenaline on opening nights can cover many mistakes. However, hard work and concentration during the weeks of rehearsals prevent even more mistakes. Real success is not left to chance. Real success in theatre depends on everyone working together as a team. Break a leg!

APPENDIX

Theatre Arts 2
Student Source Book

Six Stories and a Play

HORACE AND ALPHONSE[1]
(A Modern Folktale)

Long ago, in a far away land where the earth was hot and dry, there lived a large, old, wise iguana by the name of Alphonse. Alphonse looked very much like other iguanas who lived nearby. He had an elongated leathery green body which was covered with bumps, from his large head to the tip of his long tail. Alphonse had big round eyes and a piece of skin that flapped under his chin.

Some animals and people were afraid of Alphonse. They thought he was scary looking. "Scary? That's ridiculous!" responded Alphonse. "I am beautiful! I look just like my father and my father's father. We all were blessed with a wonderful green complexion!"

In a nearby village there lived a young hyena named Horace. Horace had a sleek coat of brown fur, four legs and a tail. Horace did not like Alphonse. He laughed at him.

Actually, Horace did not like *any* of the iguanas. He thought all iguanas were ugly. Horace made fun of their green skin and he detested their bumpy bodies and dinosaur heads. Horace chased the iguanas and tried to bite them. He told his friends that the world would be a better place if there were no iguanas. But the truth of the matter was that Horace really did not like anyone who was not a hyena.

This particular day, Horace was sprinting across the burning, dry sandy patches of earth. No rain had fallen for weeks. It was so very hot. Horace's mother had told him not to wander far from home in the noonday sun. But Horace did not always use his head. Horace wanted to run outside and play.

The sun blistered the earth's skin. Huge cracks that looked like gaping wounds broke the surface. On this day, as Horace romped and played, he tripped and fell into one of the deep tears in the ground.

Try as he might, Horace could not get his hind legs out of the narrow long cavity. Horace wiggled and squirmed. Then Horace yelled. The sun was scorching and the ground was dry. It was noontime and no one heard him. All of the animals wisely knew that they must stay in their cool safe homes until evening.

Horace cried. Horace yelped. But Horace did not laugh as he usually did. Soon Horace became silent. His throat was parched and he was terribly thirsty. Horace thought of his mother's warning. He began to cry. His mother did not know where he was.

Nearby Alphonse happened to be exploring for bugs along the burning dry earth. He heard a strange noise that sounded like a whimper. Alphonse was not familiar with that crying insect noise. He decided to explore the earth's crevices looking for the strange whimpering bug.

Alphonse searched under rocks. No crying bugs. He looked in the deep, long splits in the earth's skin. No crying bugs. After a time, Alphonse tired of looking for insects in the noonday sun. It was time to go home.

As Alphonse began to slither slowly home, he heard the muffled, quiet crying insect again. Alphonse said aloud, "I will look in just one more hollow for the crying insect. Then I must take shelter from the scorching sun."

The old iguana peered inside a huge crack and there he saw Horace! "You are not a bug!"

Horace was tired. He had worn himself out trying to get his legs free from the crevice. "Can you help me? Please?"

Alphonse looked at Horace. "Aren't you the hyena who makes fun of me and my friends? Aren't you the one who bites me and eats my friends? Why should I help you? You are not nice to me."

Horace spoke very softly for he was hot and thirsty. "I am the hyena who makes fun of you. But I am caught in this deep tear in the earth. I am going to die out here. I would not blame you if you did not help me."

Alphonse was a good iguana. He did not like to see anyone suffer. He knew that most animals who were not iguanas would suffer in the hot, dry noonday sun. Animals with fur and four legs did not often eat the juicy bugs. They would die in the heat without food and water.

Alphonse thought slowly and carefully and then devised a plan. First, he put his long tongue inside Horace's mouth and spit insect fluids. Alphonse kept spitting into the hyena's mouth for several minutes so that Horace could have a small drink of water.

Then Alphonse, who was very wise, and who had a large, leathery body, slid into the deep gash in the earth. He carefully slipped underneath Horace's entrapped legs. Then with all of his strength, Alphonse began to push and push on the hyena's legs. "Help me, Hyena. Help me get you out of this hole."

But Horace, tired from crying and squirming for such a long time, replied, "I cannot help you. I have no strength."

So Alphonse pushed and pushed with all of his iguana might. "I am an old iguana. Please try to help me." The young hyena and the old iguana together pushed and pulled on Horace's hind legs. The sun slowly moved to the west. Alphonse was very tired. He said, "Hyena, I grow weary. I fear I, too, may die in this crevice. I will try one more time to free you." So the old, wise iguana, calling forth his last strength, freed the hyena's legs.

The young hyena weakly climbed out of the crevice. Horace lay beside the hole and peered inside. Alphonse looked up at him and said, "Hyena, I am now too tired and too old to lift myself out. I think I shall just stay here and die."

Then Horace put his paw gently inside the cavity and said, "Old Iguana. You saved my life. Grab onto my paw and I will lift you." The young hyena gently lifted the wise, old iguana. "Thank you for saving my life," Horace said. "If you had not been an iguana, you would not have been able to put water in my mouth. You would not have been able to slide down that crack. Only an iguana with its leathery, bumpy body could do what you did to save my life."

"I was a stupid hyena. I made fun of anyone who was not a hyena. I did not like anyone who did not look like me or act like me. But a hyena could not have saved my life today. Only an iguana could have saved my life. Old iguana, you gave me more than my life today. You gave me some of your wisdom. Thank you."

And with those words, the young hyena walked slowly home and the old iguana found shelter under a cool rock. And to this day, I hear that no friends or relatives of Horace the hyena ever made fun of or bit or ate another iguana in their neighborhood.

Some folks say that this story is just pretend. But Alphonse told me to tell you that it is true.

THE OLD MAN AND HIS AFFECTIONATE SON[2]
(Japanese Folktale)

Once upon a time, there lived a son who was very dutiful and devoted to his father. In those days, it is said, there was a law requiring aged parents, who could no longer work, to be carried to and discarded in the mountains.

The affectionate son's father grew old and was no longer able to work. Now that the time came to discard him, the son one day set out with the father on his back and went deep into the mountains. While being carried on the son's back, the father who loved him dearly, tore off twigs of trees and dropped them to the ground as guiding marks for fear the son might get lost on his way back.

Far up in a mountain, the son spread leaves at a spot which was sheltered from the rain and placed the father on the leaves. "Now, my dear father," he said, "I must bid you farewell." Thereupon, the father broke off a nearby twig, and showing it to the son, said: "Dear son, lest you should lose your way, I have dropped twigs like this on the ground so that you may find you way. The twigs will guide you home. Now, good-bye, dear son!"

Moved to tears by his father's affection, the son could not leave him behind and carried him back down the mountain.

However, if this became known to the lord of the country, both the parent and the son would be severely punished. So the son dug a cave in the backyard and hid his father there. Every day, he carried meals to his father in the cave, and whenever he obtained a delicacy, he never failed to share it with him.

One day, the lord put up notices in various parts of the country, calling upon the people to submit "ropes made of ashes." Everybody was at a loss how to twist ashes into ropes, and in the village where the dutiful son lived, no one could solve this difficult problem, either.

Upon learning of this, the father said to his son: "Strand a rope tightly and burn it on a board." When the son did just as the father had told him to, a rope of ashes was formed. He took it to the lord and received high praise for having solved the difficult problem.

Shortly after that, the lord showed him a simple wooden pole which retained no traces of its original shape, and ordered him to confirm which end of the pole had been the root. The son brought the pole back home and asked his father what to do. The father said to him: "Put the pole slowly into the water. The end which floats lightly is the head, and the end which tends to dip into the water is the root."

The son tested the pole according to his father's instruction and reported the result to the lord. Impressed with the fine settlement of the second difficult problem as well, the lord warmly praised the son.

[2]Reprinted from FOLK TALES OF OLD JAPAN published by The Japan Times, Ltd., Tokyo, Japan. Copyright © 1975 by The Japan Times, Ltd.

However, the lord then came up with a third knotty problem, which was more difficult than the previous two. That is, he ordered the son to make a "drum that can be sounded even without beating."

The son again consulted his father, who immediately replied: "Well, nothing could be easier, son. Go and buy leather. Then go to the mountain and bring a beehive." The son did as instructed and the father made him a drum with the beehive in it. "Take this to the lord," he said to the son.

Promptly, the son took the drum to the lord. When the lord touched the drum, the surprised bees within flew about and bumped into the leather membranes. Consequently, the drum started to sound.

Complimenting the son on the remarkable solution of the three difficult problems in succession, the lord asked him how he could manage to find such wonderful solutions.

The son replied: "Being too young to have enough experience and wisdom, I could not work out any of the problems. To tell the truth, I obtained all the solutions from my old father, rich in experience and wisdom." Tearfully, he confided everything, saying: "I could not leave my father behind in the mountain, so I have hidden him in my home."

Impressed with the son's story, the lord said: "Well, I did not know old people were so sagacious and valuable. From now on, nobody will be allowed to cast off old parents in the mountains." After all, it is said, old people spent happy lives together with their young.

ANANSI AND THE HAT-SHAKING DANCE
(Africa)

Anansi the trickster, is a folk hero to the Ashanti people of West Africa. He also lives in Central America, the Caribbean and wherever people tell of his adventures. Sometimes he is a man; sometimes a spider. Sometimes he helps others; sometimes he helps himself. But at all times he is extremely *clever*. "More clever than all the rest of the world put together," say the storytellers from Africa.

Anansi, himself, loved to boast that he could do anything *better* than the other animals of the jungle "When it comes to eating, I can eat twice as much as anyone else. Or I can hold my breath twice as long. Or walk twice as far, or dance twice as vigorously." And because he boasted twice as loudly, others would say they believed him — just to gain a little peace and quiet.

There were times, however, when some of Anansi's schemes didn't turn out the way he planned them. That was the case with his hat-shaking dance.

This story takes place in the old days when Anansi sported a full head of hair and wore a tall hat to show off how handsome he was. One afternoon, news arrived from a nearby village that Anansi's mother-in-law had died. His wife, Aso, gathered some clothes, and set off for her village to attend the funeral. Anansi told Aso, "I will follow in a few hours. I must prepare my mourning clothing."

What Anansi was *really* preparing, however, was how he might show that he could mourn his mother-in-law twice as much as any other mourner. He decided he would do it by refusing to eat anything for eight days. Knowing he could never truly last that long without food, Anansi made himself a huge meal after Aso departed. Then, putting on his mourning clothes and tall hat, he went to join his wife.

The funeral was held the next day. Afterwards a beautiful table of meats and fruits was spread out for the mourners. As was the custom, everyone filled their plates: the rabbit, the snake, the porcupine, and naturally, Aso, herself. But Anansi put up his hands and said, "I cannot properly mourn for my mother-in-law and fill my stomach with rich food from the funeral feast."

The guineafowl said, "Mourners are not required to fast after the death of a loved one. Please join us. This is a proper feast."

"You go ahead," said Anansi, "but I shall follow the customs of my own village and not eat for eight days." Though the food smelled delicious, he wanted more than anything to prove that he was the greatest mourner at the funeral.

On the second day the funeral feast included hot steaming yams, one of Anansi's favorite dishes. Aso said, "Eat, dear husband. There is no need for you to fast."

"No, no," Anansi protested. "What kind of a son-in-law do you think I am? I will not eat for eight days." Yet those yams *did* smell good. And he was *ever* so hungry.

On the third day the feast tables displayed crisp vegetables, more varieties of yams and fresh sweet coconut. Anansi's stomach churned inside his belly. He wanted so much to eat the food. But he said he would fast for eight days, and that is what the other mourners would see.

By the end of the third day, however, Anansi knew he would have to eat something when the villagers were not looking.

On the fourth day the rabbit, the guineafowl, the snake, and the porcupine went for a morning walk. Aso had gone to the river to wash out some bowls. So Anansi was alone near the fire where a great pot of beans was simmering and bubbling. The aroma of the cooking beans was more than he could bear.

"I'll take some to a quiet place outside the village," he thought. "No one will see me eating the beans there. I can just say that I, too, went for a walk. A longer one than anyone else took." So, while he was still alone, Anansi picked up a ladle and scooped out a huge portion of hot beans. He was looking for a dish when he heard the other villagers returning with Aso.

Anansi poured the beans into his hat, replaced the ladle, and put the hat on his head. The others came over to the pot and filled their freshly washed bowls. "Will you not break your fast today, Anansi?" said the rabbit. "Surely, you must be very hungry."

"What, and dishonor the memory of my mother-in-law?" said the trickster.

The hot beans were burning under his hat. So he put both hands to the brim, held fast, and jiggled his head. He wanted to take off the hat, but then his friends would see the beans. The beans burned more, and Anansi jumped up and down. The others looked at him strangely. So he said, "I just remembered. Today is the day of the hat shaking festival in my village. They shake and jiggle their hats like this. I do it, too, to honor the festival!"

The hot beans continued to burn his head. So Anansi jumped up and down and jiggled his hat even more furiously. In great pain, he now shouted, "I must go to the great festival in my village. I will return tomorrow." He started down the pathway, still jumping and pushing his hat back and forth.

But the others followed. "Eat something to give you strength on the journey," said the guineafowl.

"Especially if you plan on doing the hat-shaking dance all the way home," added the rabbit.

By then Anansi could stand the heat no more. He pulled his hat off his head. And the rabbit saw, and the guineafowl saw, and all the others saw the beans sticking to Anansi's head. They stood for a moment in amazement. Then they began to laugh. They pointed, and jeered, and roared.

Filled with shame, Anansi leaped into the tall grass. "Hide me!" he pleaded. And the grass out of pity did so. That is why, even today, you will find spiders hidden in the tall grass where Anansi hid in shame. That is also why Anansi's head is bald. All his beautiful hair was burned off by the hot beans he had placed under his hat.

Now, if you think Anansi learned his lesson, you are sadly mistaken. He continues to boast that he is *better* than others. And he *still* plays tricks on his neighbors to this very day.

THE GREAT WHITE STALLION
(American Frontier)

This is a story of the American frontier when settlers were traveling west across the great plains. It is also a story about the horses who lived wild and free on those plains almost 200 years ago.

Among them was a great white stallion whose beauty and majesty was legendary among the Indians. Their name for him was *Moonburst,* for his silky white coat flickered in the midnight sky as he galloped across the rolling plains. Sometimes the great white stallion frolicked with fellow companions. More often he traveled alone.

Settlers going west usually piled their belongings into a wagon and, for protection, joined with other families in a caravan called a wagon train. One group heading toward Texas was guided by a wagon master named Albert. His wife had died the previous winter, so Albert brought along his four-year-old daughter on the arduous trip. Her name was Gretchen.

As the wagon train moved forward, Gretchen's father sometimes allowed her to ride on a gentle mare. The mare also carried cornmeal sacks for the travelers. To make sure that Gretchen didn't fall off the horse, her father tied her legs to the cornmeal sacks.

One afternoon, a group of wild horses galloped past the slow moving wagon train. Leading them was the great white stallion who the Indians called *Moonburst.* Gretchen's mare caught sight of the magnificent beast and had an uncontrollable yearning to follow him. She wandered off from the rear of the wagon train. Albert, who was at the front of the procession, did not notice that his daughter was missing.

The mare headed northward where the wild horses had gone. Once separated from the humans, she quickened her pace, hoping to get another glimpse of the beautiful white stallion. But the gentle mare had little chance to catch up with her unbridled brethren. At nightfall, she and her rider came to rest near a thicket. They were exhausted, alone and lost.

Suddenly, a group of wild mares burst out of the thicket and surrounded the twosome. These were not the young horses that had romped nearby in the afternoon. They were *mean.* They were fierce. And they were *hungry.* Closing in on the girl and her horse, they tore at the cornmeal bags strapped to the mare's back. Gretchen was terrified, and she screamed for help. But there was no one within miles to hear her.

The wild mares ripped the bags open with their teeth and bruised the little girl's legs in their fury. Gretchen cried out louder. She could not escape the hungry mares for she was still securely bound to the meal sacks.

Then a wild and piercing bray drowned out all the other noises rumbling in that evening sky. Gretchen turned and saw the great white stallion, up on his two hind legs, looking and sounding like a warrior god. The attackers saw him, too. They turned and sped off into the thicket while Gretchen's mare stood her ground. Once the wild mares were gone, Gretchen, herself, was strangely quiet and no longer alarmed.

His main mission accomplished, the great white stallion settled onto all four legs, approached Gretchen, and gently gnawed at the ropes that bound her to the mare. After freeing her, he took her jacket collar in his mouth and lifted her tenderly to the ground. Then the great white stallion made a satisfied snort and galloped away into the night.

Though shaken by the events of the day, the girl was also tired. She laid her head on a tuft of grass and slept soundly till morning. When the sun came up, however, Gretchen and her mare were still alone, still lost. And there was no way Gretchen could remount her horse. She stayed near the mare and searched the plains in all directions, hoping her father would rescue her. But no one came, and the sun began to set.

As the western sky turned a brilliant red, the great white stallion galloped into view along the southern horizon. He came straight toward the girl and her horse. In the sunset, his silky white coat flashed like red lightning on the darkening plain. The stallion halted near the two lost wanderers. He lifted Gretchen up onto the mare's back and nudged the gentle animal toward the last rays of twilight.

Guiding the mare throughout the night, the stallion crossed a river and brought horse and child to within a mile of the sleeping wagon train settlers. He next showed the mare how to follow the river bank. Then, at a sharp bend in the shoreline, he suddenly stopped. When his companions stopped, too, the stallion nodded his head to the south and neighed as if giving a command. His message was clear: they should continue on. And so they did.

When the mare and her rider reached the settlers' camp, Gretchen's father was overjoyed. He and his followers had spent the whole day and half the night searching for his daughter. The girl hugged her daddy and told him about the miraculous rescue by the magnificent great white stallion.

For many years afterwards, pioneers traveling across the plains always scanned the horizons for a glimpse of the horse the Indians called *Moonburst*. Some claimed they saw him. But no one ever again had an adventure that was as frightening, or as inspiring, as the journey of Gretchen and her mare.

PANDORA'S BOX
(Greek Mythology)

According to ancient Greek storytellers, Pandora was the first mortal woman on Earth. In Greek her name means "all-gifted." This is an appropriate name for Pandora, for she was created by the great god Zeus as a gift for Epimetheus. Moreover, at Zeus' command, each of the other gods gave Pandora a gift. From Athena came knowledge in the arts; from Aphrodite, beauty. Hermes gave her cunning, and all the rest helped make Pandora a talented and attractive mortal. She was truly "all-gifted."

However, Zeus was angry with Epimetheus and his brother, Prometheus, for having given man fire from the gods. So his gift of Pandora was, in part, a scheme to cause troubles for mankind. The gods had not only given Pandora many fine attributes, they also presented her with a beautiful golden box. She was told to keep the box close by, but *never* to open it. And Pandora was given one more trait: *curiosity*.

Epimetheus had been warned by Prometheus not to accept any offerings from Zeus. But when he beheld the exquisite Pandora, he was unable to refuse such a magnificent gift. So Pandora became his wife.

When she came to live with Epimetheus, she showed him the box. She told him that neither she nor anyone else was *ever* permitted to peek inside. Yet she also confessed that she often wondered what was *so* valuable that it was stored in such a precious container. She also questioned aloud why this box was so different that no one was ever to set his eyes on the treasures inside.

"The gods don't have to give you reasons," said Epimetheus. "Their warnings are reason enough. Even now my brother is being punished because he displeased Zeus. Be careful not to make the same kind of mistake that he did."

Her husband's warning was forceful enough to make Pandora hold back her curiosity, for a while. But a week later as she walked by the box, it seemed to her that a ray of sunlight had singled out the container. The sunlight made its golden surface glisten. Was the box *beckoning* to her?

She stepped closer to the box and examined its surface. There was nothing evil looking about it. The hammered gold side panels were simply joined at each edge with a sturdy piece of silver trim. Hinges secured the lid at the back. And a large hasp in the front fit over a U-shaped staple. The hasp, in turn, was held in place by a golden cord which was knotted in a most unusual pattern.

"Epimetheus says that Zeus will be angry," Pandora reasoned to herself. "But *why* did the gods give me this box in the first place? And why have I been given the gift of curiosity? Maybe Zeus *wants* me to open the box."

She looked at the knot holding down the hasp. She knew that, with her cunning, she would have no problem untying it. Then she thought to herself again. "The gods' instructions were clear. I am *not* allowed to look inside. Surely, I am in more danger of angering them than I am likely to please them. I will *not* open the box."

So Pandora turned and started to walk away. But she had taken no more than two steps when she stopped and spoke her thoughts out loud. "What's the use. Eventually I must know what is in the box. I might as well open it *now.*"

Determined, she walked quickly to the box. Skillfully, Pandora untied the knot on the hasp, and lifted the lid. Out flew bats, hornets, flies, and other ghastly winged creatures! They were so numerous and varied that they blackened the room with their buzzing bodies. Pandora screamed in horror. Instinctively, she knew that the flying gremlins symbolized the evils, diseases, worries, and troubles that would forever fly across the paths of all mankind. They would multiply and change in form. Man might conquer some. But others would hide in dark corners and cause him grief throughout the rest of history.

Hardly a second had passed before Pandora realized the mean trick that Zeus had played. She quickly swung the box lid closed. But the damage had been done. At that moment Epimetheus, who had heard Pandora scream, came into the house. Spying the winged creatures, he realized what must have happened. But he blamed Zeus more than he did his wife. The ruler of the gods knew that Pandora's curiosity would lead to this curse on all humans.

Epimetheus comforted his frightened wife and helped her tie down the hasp on the lid. As they stood next to each other, both heard a tiny voice inside the box: "Please, let me out! I can help you."

Husband and wife looked at each other. "That isn't the voice of a demon," said Pandora. "What should we do?"

"Let me out *please*!" the voice repeated.

"Who are you?" asked Pandora.

"Let me out and you will see. I am something all humans need, especially now that the world is filled with disease and evil thoughts."

Pandora, who sensed that the voice was telling the truth, looked again at her husband. She wanted to know who the creature inside the box could possibly be. But would her *curiosity* once again lead to ruin?

"Open the lid," said her husband. "One more trouble in the swarm you have already loosed upon the world cannot make any difference." So Pandora lifted the lid once again. Out fluttered a single butterfly, brightening the air with its vivid colors.

"Ah! You have already chased away some of the gloom," said Pandora. "Who are you?"

"I am called *Hope*," said the butterfly. "I was placed in the box to help you deal with all the demons you released. Whenever you feel burdened with the problems or ills or troubles, just remember: there is always *hope.*"

So Pandora's *curiosity* is partly responsible for the sorrows we experience in life. But we must also thank her for her gift to mankind: the gift of *hope.*

THE OLD RAT AND THE YOUNG RAT
(A Fable)

One bright, sunny morning, a young rat happily crawled out of his hole into the kitchen. There he spied a piece of cheese! The wondrous smell of the cheese overpowered him. He began to take a nibble and...SNAP! He was caught in a trap! The day no longer seemed bright and sunny. The young rat was very sad, indeed. Then he saw an old rat out for a stroll, and his heart leaped with joy. "Help! he shouted. "I am caught in this trap. Please help!"

The old rat stopped and looked. But he came no closer to the young rat. "Why do you call on me?" he said. "Surely, you do not think I am to blame for your troubles?"

"Oh, no," said the young rat. "But *please* help me."

"Clever rats know how to solve their own problems," said the old rat. "What do you want from me?"

"Find a big match and push it under the metal spring," the young rat pleaded. "If you put the match stick right here next to my leg, I could help you push it up. If we raise the spring just a tiny bit, I am sure I can escape."

"Why should I help?" said the old rat. "Look for a rat who owes you a favor, and ask him for help." He started to walk away. Then he stopped and turned. "And let me give you some advice. Wise rats stay clear of traps." The old rat turned once more and went on his way.

Wriggling and squirming with great effort, the young rat finally managed to get free. He wrapped a torn scrap of cloth around his leg and proceeded about his business.

The next day he was still limping, but it was, again, a bright and sunny morning. So the young rat cautiously ventured out into the parlor. As he rounded a corner, he spied a huge cat with something flattened beneath its paw. Keeping his distance, the young rat looked more closely and realized the "something" was the old rat.

When the old rat saw the young rat, he shouted, "Help me, little rat! This cat has captured me, and I do not think he is going to let me go!"

"Why do you call on me?" said the young rat. "I am not to blame for your trouble."

"I know that," whined the old rat. "But *please* help me!"

"Clever rats know how to solve their own problems," said the young rat. "What do you want from me?"

"Listen," whispered the old rat. "Go around to the back of the cat and tickle his tail. He will forget about me and try to catch you. Then we can both escape."

"I would help," said the young rat, "but I have too much to lose and little to gain. It is too bad you did not give me assistance when I needed it. I would have done anything I could to pay you back. Now you must find a rat who owes you a favor, and ask him for help." He started to walk away. Then he stopped and turned. "And let me give you some advice. Wise rats stay clear of cats."

Moral: Be kind to fellow creatures, for you never know when you may need their kindness in return.

BOX AND COX
by John Madison Morton

(The scene is a decently furnished room in London. A canopy bed stands Up Center with its curtains pulled closed. Also visible On-stage are a window, a fireplace with mantelpiece and three doors. Other items in the room include a table, two chairs, and a chest of drawers. When the scene opens, COX, in his shirtsleeves, is viewing his hair in a small looking glass that he holds in his hand.)

COX:	I've half a mind to register an oath that I'll never have my hair cut again! *(His hair is very short.)* I look as if I had just been cropped for the militia! And I was particularly emphatic in my instructions to the hair-dresser, only to cut the ends off. He must have thought I meant the other ends! Never mind. I shan't meet anybody to care about so early. Eight o'clock, I declare! I haven't a moment to lose. Fate has placed me with the most punctual, particular, and peremptory[1] of hatters, and I must fulfill my destiny. *(Knock at hall door)* Open locks, whoever knocks! *(Enter MRS. BOUNCER.)*
MRS. B.:	Good morning, Mr. Cox. I hope you slept comfortably, Mr. Cox?
COX:	I can't say I did, Mrs. B. I should feel obliged to you, if you could accommodate me with a more protuberant bolster,[2] Mrs. B. The one I've got now seems to me to have about a handful and a half of feathers at each end, and nothing whatever in the middle.
MRS. B.:	Anything to accommodate you, Mr. Cox.
COX:	Thank you. Then, perhaps, you'll be good enough to hold this glass, while I finish my toilet.[3]
MRS. B.:	Certainly. *(Holding glass before COX, who ties his cravat.)* Why, I do declare, you've had your hair cut.
COX:	Cut? It strikes me I've had it mowed! It's very kind of you to mention it, but I'm sufficiently conscious of the absurdity of my personal appearance already. *(Puts on his coat.)* Now for my hat. *(Puts on his hat, which comes over his eyes.)* That's the effect of having one's hair cut. This hat fitted me quite tight before. Luckily I've got two to three more. *(Goes into closet, and returns with three hats of different shapes, and puts them on, one after the other. All are too big for him.)* This is pleasant! Never mind. This one appears to me to wabble about rather less than the others. *(Puts on hat.)* And now I'm off! By the bye, Mrs. Bouncer, I wish to call your attention to a fact that has been evident to me for some time past, and that is that my coals go remarkably fast.
MRS. B.:	Lor, Mr. Cox!
COX:	It is not the case only with the coals, Mrs. Bouncer, but I've lately observed a gradual and steady increase of evaporation among my candles, wood, sugar, and lucifer matches.[4]
MRS. B.:	Lor, Mr. Cox! You surely don't suspect me!
COX:	I don't say I do, Mrs. B., only I wish you distinctly to understand that I

[1]demanding
[2]thicker pillow
[3]morning grooming
[4]sulfur matches

don't believe it's the cat.

MRS. B.:	Is there anything else you've got to grumble about, sir?
COX:	Grumble! Mrs. Bouncer, do you possess such a thing as a dictionary?
MRS. B.:	No, sir.
COX:	Then I'll lend you one, and if you turn to the letter G, you'll find "Grumble, verb neuter: to complain without a cause." Now that's not my case, Mrs. B., and now that we are upon the subject I wish to know how it is that I frequently find my apartment full of smoke?
MRS. B.:	Why — I suppose the chimney.
COX:	The chimney doesn't smoke tobacco. I'm speaking of tobacco smoke, Mrs. B. I hope, Mrs. Bouncer, you aren't guilty of cheroots or Cubas?[5]
MRS. B.:	Not I, indeed, Mr. Cox.
COX:	Nor partial to a pipe?
MRS. B.:	No, sir.
COX:	Then, how is that —
MRS. B.:	Why — I suppose — yes, that must be it.
COX:	At present I am entirely of your opinion — because I haven't the most distant particle of an idea what you mean.
MRS. B.:	Why the gentleman who has got the attics is hardly ever without a pipe in his mouth. And there he sits, with his feet upon the mantelpiece.
COX:	The mantelpiece! That strikes me as being a considerable stretch, either of your imagination, Mrs. B, or the gentleman's legs. I presume you mean the fender or the hob.
MRS. B.:	Sometimes one, sometimes t'other. Well, there he sits for hours, and puffs away into the fireplace.
COX:	Ah, then you mean to say that this gentleman's smoke, instead of emulating the example of all other sorts of smoke, and going up the chimney, thinks proper to affect a singularity by taking the contrary direction?
MRS. B.:	Why —
COX:	Then, I suppose, the gentleman you are speaking of is the same individual that I invariably meet coming upstairs when I'm going down, and going downstairs when I'm coming up!
MRS. B.:	Why — yes — I —
COX:	From the appearance of his outward manner, I should unhesitatingly set him down as a gentleman connected with the printing interest.
MRS. B.:	Yes, sir — and a very respectable young gentleman he is.
COX:	Well, good morning, Mrs. Bouncer.

[5]cigars

MRS. B.:	You'll be back at your usual time, I suppose, sir?
COX:	Yes, nine o'clock. You needn't light my fire in the future, Mrs. B. I'll do it myself. Don't forget the bolster! *(Going, stops.)* A halfpenny worth of milk, Mrs. Bouncer. And be good enough to let it stand. I wish the cream to accumulate. *(He exits.)*
MRS. B.:	He's gone at last! I declare I was all in a tremble for fear Mr. Box would come in before Mr. Cox went out. Luckily, they've never met yet. And what's more they're not very likely to do so; for Mr. Box is hard at work at a newspaper office all night, and doesn't come home till the morning, and Mr. Cox is busy making hats all day long, and doesn't come home till night; so that I'm getting double rent for my room, and neither of my lodgers are any the wiser for it. It was a capital idea of mine — that it was! But I haven't an instant to lose. First of all, let me put Mr. Cox's things out of Mr. Box's way. *(She takes the three hats, COX's dressing gown and slippers, opens door at left and puts them in, then shuts door and locks it.)* Now then, to put the key where Mr. Cox always finds it. *(Puts the key on the ledge of the door.)* I really must beg Mr. Box not to smoke so much. I was so dreadfully puzzled to know what to say when Mr. Cox spoke about it. Now then, to make the bed — and don't let me forget that what's the head of the bed for Mr. Cox becomes the foot of the bed for Mr. Box. People's tastes do differ so. *(She goes behind the curtains of the bed, and seems to be making it — then appears with a very thin bolster in her hand.)* The idea of Mr. Cox presuming to complain of such a bolster as this! *(She disappears again behind curtains.)*
BOX:	*(Outside the door)* Pooh-pooh! Why don't you keep your own side of the staircase, sir? *(Enters, dressed as a printer. Puts his head out at door again, shouting.)* It was as much your fault as mine, sir! I say, sir, it was as much your fault as mine, sir!
MRS. B.:	*(Emerging from behind the curtains of bed)* Lor, Mr. Box! What is the matter?
BOX:	Mind your own business, Bouncer!
MRS. B.:	Dear, dear, Mr. Box! What a temper you are in, to be sure! I declare you're quite pale in the face!
BOX:	What color would you have a man be, who has been setting up long leaders[6] for a daily paper all night?
MRS. B.:	But then you've all the day to yourself.
BOX:	*(Looking significantly at MRS. BOUNCER)* So it seems! Far be it from me, Bouncer, to hurry your movements, but I think it right to acquaint you with my immediate intention of divesting myself of my garments, and going to bed.
MRS. B.:	Oh, Mr. Box!
BOX:	Stop! Can you inform me who the individual is that I invariably encounter going downstairs when I'm coming up, and coming upstairs when I'm going down?
MRS. B.:	*(Confused)* Oh — yes — the gentleman in the attic, sir.
BOX:	Oh! There's nothing particularly remarkable about him, except his hats. I meet him in all sorts of hats — white hats and black hats — hats with broad

[6]lines of type

brims, and hats with narrow brims — hats with naps, and hats without naps. In short, I have come to the conclusion, that he must be individually and professionally associated with the hatting interest.

MRS. B.: Yes, sir. And, by the bye, Mr. Box, he begged me to request of you, as a particular favor, that you would not smoke quite so much.

BOX: Did he? Then you may tell the gentle hatter, with my compliments, that if he objects to the effluvia[7] of tobacco, he had better domesticate himself in some adjoining parish.

MRS. B.: *(Pathetically)* Oh, Mr. Box! You surely wouldn't deprive me of a lodger?

BOX: It would come to precisely the same thing, Bouncer, because if I detect the slightest attempt to put my pipe out, I at once give you warning that I shall give you warning at once.

MRS. B.: Well, Mr. Box, do you want anything more of me?

BOX: On the contrary, I've had quite enough of you!

MRS. B.: Well, if ever! What next, I wonder? *(Goes out slamming door after her.)*

BOX: It's quite extraordinary, the trouble I always have to get rid of that venerable female! She knows I'm up all night, and yet she seems to set her face against my indulging in a horizontal position by day. Now, let me see — shall I take my nap before I swallow my breakfast, or shall I take my breakfast before I swallow my nap? — I mean, shall I swallow my nap before — No, never mind! I've got a rasher[8] of bacon somewhere. *(Feeling in his pockets)* I've the most distinct and vivid recollection of having purchased a rasher of bacon — Oh, here it is. *(Produces it, wrapped in paper, and places it on table.)* And a penny roll. The next thing is to light the fire. Where are my lucifers?[9] *(Looking on mantelpiece and taking box, opens it.)* Now, 'pon my life, this is too bad of Bouncer — this is, by several degrees, too bad! I had a whole box full, three days ago, and now there's only one! I'm perfectly aware that she purloins[10] my coals and my candles, and my sugar, but I did think — oh, yes, I did think that my lucifers would be sacred! *(Takes candlestick off the mantelpiece. In it there is a very small stub of a candle which he looks at.)* Now I should like to ask any unprejudiced person or persons their opinion touching this candle. In the first place, a candle is an article that I don't require because I'm only at home in the day time, and I bought this candle on the first of May — Chimney-Sweepers' Day — calculating that it would last me three months, and here's one week not half over, and the candle three parts gone. *(Lights the fire. Then takes down a gridiron,[11] which is hanging over the fireplace.)* Mrs. Bouncer has been using my gridiron! The last article of consumption that I cooked upon it was a pork chop, and now it is powerfully impregnated with the odour of red herrings! *(Places gridiron on fire, and then, with fork, lays rasher of bacon on the gridiron.)* How sleepy I am, to be sure! I'd indulge myself with a nap, if there was anybody here to superintend the turning of my bacon. *(Yawning again)* Perhaps it will turn itself. I must lie down — so, here goes. *(Lies in the bed, closing the curtain around him. After a short pause enter COX hurriedly.)*

COX: Well, wonders will never cease! Conscious of being eleven minutes, and a half behind time, I was sneaking into the shop, in a state of considerable

[7]unpleasant smell
[8]small amount (2 or 3 slices)
[9]matches
[10]steals
[11]a cooking grate used over a fire

excitement, when my venerable employer, with a smile of extreme benevolence on his aged countenance, said to me, "Cox, I shan't want you today. You can have a holiday." Thoughts of "Gravesend and back — fare, One Shilling," — instantly suggested themselves, intermingled with visions of "Greenwich for Fourpence!" Then came the Two-Penny Omnibuses, and the Half-penny boats — in short, I'm quite bewildered! However, I must have my breakfast. That'll give me time to reflect. I've bought a mutton chop, so I shan't want any dinner. *(Puts chop on table.)* Good gracious! I've forgot the bread. Holloa![12] What's this? A roll, I declare! Come, that's lucky! Now then to light the fire. Holloa! *(Seeing the lucifer box on table)* Who presumes to touch my box of lucifers? Why, it's empty! I left one in it. I'll take my oath I did. Heyday! Why, the fire is lighted! Where's the gridiron? On the fire, I declare! And what's that on it? Bacon! Bacon it is! Well now, 'pon my life, there's a quiet coolness about Mrs. Bouncer's proceedings that's almost amusing. She takes my last lucifer, my coals, and my gridiron, to cook her breakfast by! No, no — I can't stand this! Come out of that! *(Pokes fork into bacon, and puts it on a plate on the table, then places his chop on the gridiron, which he puts on the fire.)* Now then, for my breakfast things... *(Taking key hung up, opens door, and goes out slamming the door after him, with a loud noise.)*

BOX: *(Suddenly showing his head from behind the curtains)* Come in! If it's you, Mrs. Bouncer, you needn't be afraid. I wonder how long I've been asleep? *(Suddenly recollecting)* Goodness gracious, my bacon! *(Leaps off bed and runs to the fireplace.)* Holloa! What's this? A chop! Whose chop? Mrs. Bouncer's I'll be bound. She thought to cook her breakfast while I was asleep — with my coals, too — and my gridiron! Ha! But where's my bacon? *(Seeing it on table)* Here it is. Well, 'pon my life, Bouncer's doing it! And shall I curb my indignation? Shall I falter in my vengeance? No! *(Digs the fork into the chop, opens window, and throws chop out, shutting window.)* So much for Bouncer's breakfast, and now for my own! *(With the fork he puts the bacon on the gridiron again.)* I may as well lay my breakfast things. *(Goes to mantelpiece, takes key out of one of the ornaments, opens door, and exits, slamming door after him.)*

COX: *(Putting his head in another door)* Come in — come in! *(Enters with a small tray of tea things which he places on dresser and suddenly recollects.)* Oh, goodness! My chop! *(Running to fireplace)* Holloa — what's...? The bacon again! Oh, pooh! Zounds — confound it — dash it — damn it — I can't stand this! *(Pokes fork into bacon, opens window, and flings it out, shuts window again, returns to dresser for tea things, and encounters BOX coming from his cupboard with his tea things. They walk Downstage Center together.)* Who are you, sir?

BOX: If you come to that, who are you?

COX: What do you want here, sir?

BOX: If you come to that, what do you want?

COX: *(Aside)* It's the printer! *(Puts tea things on a chair.)*

BOX: *(Aside)* It's the hatter! *(Puts tea things on table.)*

COX: Go to your attic, sir —

BOX: My attic, sir! Your attic, sir!

[12]Hello! (an exclamation of surprise)

COX:	Printer, I shall do you a frightful injury, if you don't instantly leave my apartment.
BOX:	Your apartment? You mean my apartment, you contemptible[13] hatter, you!
COX:	Your apartment? Ha! ha! — Come, I like that! Look here, sir — *(Produces a paper out of his pocket.)* Mrs. Bouncer's receipt for the last week's rent, sir.
BOX:	*(Produces a paper, and holds it close to COX's face.)* Ditto, sir!
COX:	*(Suddenly shouting)* Thieves!
BOX:	Murder!
BOX and COX:	Mrs. Bouncer! *(Each runs to door, calling. MRS. BOUNCER runs in at door.)*
MRS. B.:	What is the matter? *(COX and BOX seize MRS. BOUNCER by the arm and drag her forward.)*
BOX:	Instantly remove that hatter!
COX:	Immediately turn out that printer!
MRS. B.:	Well — but, gentlemen —
COX:	Explain! *(Pulling her round to him)*
BOX:	Explain! *(Pulling her round to him)* Whose room is this?
COX:	Yes, woman, whose room is this?
BOX:	Doesn't it belong to me?
MRS. B.:	No!
COX:	There! You hear, sir — it belongs to me!
MRS. B.:	*(Sobbing)* No, it belongs to both of you!
COX and BOX:	Both of us?!
MRS. B.:	Oh, dear gentlemen, don't be angry, but you see, this gentleman *(Pointing to BOX)* only being at home in the daytime, and that gentleman *(Pointing to COX)* at night, I thought I might venture, until my little back second floor room was ready —
BOX and COX:	*(Eagerly)* When will your little back second floor room be ready?
MRS. B.:	Why, tomorrow.
COX:	I'll take it!
BOX:	So will I!
MRS. B.:	Excuse me, but if you both take it, you may just as well stop where you are.
COX and BOX:	True.
COX:	I spoke first, sir.
BOX:	With all my heart, sir, the little back second floor room is yours, sir. Now, go!

[13]worthless

COX:	Go? Pooh-pooh!
MRS. B.:	Now don't quarrel, gentlemen. You see, there used to be a partition here.
COX and BOX:	Then put it up!
MRS. B.:	Nay, I'll see if I can't get the other room ready this very day. Now do keep your tempers. *(Exits.)*
COX:	What a disgusting position! *(Walking rapidly around stage)*
BOX:	*(Sitting down on a chair at one side of table, and following COX's movements)* Will you allow me to observe, if you have not had any exercise today, you'd better go out and take it.
COX:	I shall not do anything of the sort, sir. *(Seating himself at the table opposite BOX)*
BOX:	Very well, sir.
COX:	Very well, sir! However, don't let me prevent you from going out.
BOX:	Don't flatter yourself, sir. *(COX is about to break a piece of the roll off.)* Holloa! That's my roll, sir — *(Snatches it away, puts a pipe in his mouth, lights it with a piece of tinder, and puffs smoke across to COX.)*
COX:	Holloa! What are you about, sir?
BOX:	What am I about? I'm about to smoke.
COX:	Whew! *(Goes and opens window at BOX's back.)*
BOX:	Holloa! *(Turns around.)* Put down that window, sir!
COX:	Then put your pipe out, sir!
BOX:	There!
COX:	There! *(Slams down window, and re-seats himself.)*
BOX:	I shall retire to my pillow. *(Goes up, takes off his jacket, then goes toward bed, and sits down upon it.)*
COX:	*(Jumps up, goes to bed, and lies down at right of BOX.)* I beg your pardon, sir. I cannot allow anyone to rumple my bed. *(Both rising)*
BOX:	Your bed? Hark ye, sir, can you fight?
COX:	No, sir.
BOX:	No? Then come on. *(Sparring at COX.)*
COX:	Sit down, sir, or I'll instantly vociferate[14] "Police!"
BOX:	*(Seats himself on bed. COX does the same.)* I say, sir.
COX:	Well, sir?
BOX:	Although we are doomed to occupy the same room for a few hours longer, I don't see any necessity for our cutting each other's throats, sir.
COX:	Not at all. It's an operation that I should decidedly object to.

BOX: *(Rises.)* **And after all, I have no violent animosity to you, sir.**

COX: *(Rises.)* **Nor have I any rooted antipathy to you, sir.**

BOX: **Besides, it was all Mrs. Bouncer's fault, sir.**

COX: **Entirely, sir.** *(Gradually approaching chairs)*

BOX: **Very well, sir!** *(Sits.)*

COX: **Very well, sir!** *(Sits. Pause)*

BOX: **Take a bit of roll, sir?**

COX: **Thank ye, sir.** *(Breaking a bit off. Pause)*

BOX: **Do you sing, sir?**

COX: **I sometimes join in a chorus.**

BOX: **Then give us a chorus.** *(Pause)* **Have you seen the Bosjemans, sir?**

COX: **No, sir. My wife wouldn't let me.**

BOX: **Your wife!**

COX: **That is, my intended wife.**

BOX: **Well, that's the same thing! I congratulate you.** *(Shaking hands)*

COX: *(With a deep sigh)* **Thank ye.** *(Seeing BOX about to get up)* **You needn't disturb yourself, sir. She won't come here.**

BOX: **Oh! I understand. You've got a snug little establishment of your own here — on the sly. Cunning dog.** *(Nudging COX)*

COX: *(Drawing himself up)* **No such thing, sir. I repeat, sir, no such thing, sir, but my wife — I mean, my intended wife — happens to be the proprietor of a considerable number of bathing machines.**[15]

BOX: *(Suddenly)* **Ha! Where?** *(Grasping COX's arm)*

COX: **At a favorite watering-place. How curious you are!**

BOX: **Not at all. Well?**

COX: **Consequently, in the bathing season — which luckily is rather a long one — we see but little of each other; but as that is now over, I am daily indulging in the expectation of being blessed with the sight of my beloved.** *(Very seriously)* **Are you married?**

BOX: **Me? Why — not exactly!**

COX: **Ah — a happy bachelor!**

BOX: **Why — not — precisely!**

COX: **Oh! A widower?**

BOX: **No — not absolutely!**

[14]Shout
[15]small bathhouses on wheels

COX:	You'll excuse me, sir, but, at present, I don't exactly understand how you can help being one of the three.
BOX:	Not help it?
COX:	No, sir — not you, nor any other man alive!
BOX:	Ah, that may be. But I'm not alive!
COX:	*(Pushing back his chair)* You'll excuse me, sir, but I don't like joking upon such subjects.
BOX:	I'm perfectly serious, sir. I've been defunct[16] for the last three years.
COX:	*(Shouting)* Will you be quiet, sir?
BOX:	If you won't believe me, I'll refer you to a very large, numerous, and respectable circle of disconsolate friends.
COX:	My dear sir — my very dear sir — if there does exist any ingenious contrivance whereby a man on the eve of committing matrimony can leave this world, and yet stop in it, I shouldn't be sorry to know it.
BOX:	Oh! Then I presume I'm not to set you down as being frantically attached to your intended?
COX:	Why, not exactly; and yet, at present, I'm only aware of one obstacle to doting[17] upon her, and that is, that I can't abide her!
BOX:	Then there's nothing more easy. Do as I did.
COX:	*(Eagerly)* I will! What was it?
BOX:	Drown yourself!
COX:	*(Shouting again)* Will you be quiet, sir?
BOX:	Listen to me. Three years ago it was my misfortune to captivate the affections of a still blooming, though somewhat middle-aged widow, at Ramsgate.
COX:	*(Aside)* Singular enough! Just my case three months ago at Margate.
BOX:	Well, sir, to escape her importunities, I came to the determination of enlisting into the Blues, or Life Guards.
COX:	*(Aside)* So did I. How very odd!
BOX:	But they wouldn't have me — they actually had the effrontery[18] to say that I was too short.
COX:	*(Aside)* And I wasn't tall enough!
BOX:	So I was obliged to content myself with a marching regiment — I enlisted!
COX:	*(Aside)* So did I. Singular coincidence!
BOX:	I'd no sooner done so, than I was sorry for it.
COX:	*(Aside)* So was I.

[16]dead
[17]showing fond affection
[18]insulting boldness

BOX: My infatuated widow offered to purchase my discharge, on condition that I'd lead her to the altar.

COX: *(Aside)* Just my case!

BOX: I hesitated — at last I consented.

COX: *(Aside)* I consented at once!

BOX: Well, sir, the day fixed for the happy ceremony at length drew near. In fact, too near to be pleasant. So I suddenly discovered that I wasn't worthy to possess her, and I told her so — when instead of being flattered by the compliment, she flew upon me like a tiger of the female gender. I rejoined, when suddenly something whizzed past me, within an inch of my ear, and shattered into a thousand fragments against the mantelpiece. It was the slop-basin. I retaliated with a tea cup. We parted, and the next morning I was served with a notice of action for breach of promise.

COX: Well, sir?

BOX: Well, sir, ruin stared me in the face. The action proceeded against me with gigantic strides. I took a desperate resolution — I left my home early one morning, with one suit of clothes on my back, and another tied up in a bundle, under my arm. I arrived on the cliffs — opened my bundle — deposited the suit of clothes on the very verge of the precipice, took one look down into the yawning gulph beneath me, and walked off in the opposite direction.

COX: Dear me! I think I begin to have some slight perception of your meaning. Ingenious creature! You disappeared — the suit of clothes was found —

BOX: Exactly — and in one of the pockets of the coat, or the waistcoat, or the pantaloons[19] — I forget which — there was also found a piece of paper, with these affecting farewell words: "This is thy work, oh, Penelope Ann!"

COX: Penelope Ann! *(Starts up, takes BOX by the arm, and leads him slowly to front of stage.)* Penelope Ann?

BOX: Penelope Ann!

COX: Originally widow of William Wiggins?

BOX: Widow of William Wiggins!

COX: Proprietor of bathing machines?

BOX: Proprietor of bathing machines!

COX: At Margate?

BOX: And Ramsgate!

COX: It must be she! And you, sir — you are Box — the lamented, long-lost Box!

BOX: I am!

COX: And I was about to marry the interesting creature you so cruelly deceived.

BOX: Ha! Then you are Cox?

[19]trousers

COX:	I am!
BOX:	I heard of it. I congratulate you. I give you joy! And now, I think I'll go and take a stroll. *(Going)*
COX:	No you don't! *(Stopping him)* I'll not lose sight of you till I've restored you to the arms of your intended.[20]
BOX:	My intended? You mean your intended.
COX:	No, sir — yours!
BOX:	How can she be my intended, now that I'm drowned?
COX:	You're no such thing, sir! And I prefer presenting you to Penelope Ann.
BOX:	I've no wish to be introduced to your intended.
COX:	My intended? How can that be, sir? You proposed to her first!
BOX:	What of that, sir? I came to an untimely end, and you popped the question afterwards.
COX:	Very well, sir!
BOX:	Very well, sir!
COX:	You are much more worthy of her than I am, sir. Permit me, then, to follow the generous impulse of my nature. I give her up to you.
BOX:	Benevolent being! I wouldn't rob you for the world! *(Going)* Good morning, sir!
COX:	*(Seizing him)* Stop!
BOX:	Unhand me, hatter! Or I shall cast off the lamb and assume the lion!
COX:	Pooh! *(Snapping his fingers close to BOX's face)*
BOX:	An insult! To my very face — under my very nose! *(Rubbing it)* You know the consequences, sir — instant satisfaction, sir!
COX:	With all my heart, sir! *(They go to the fireplace and begin ringing bells violently, and pull down bell-pulls.)*
BOX and COX:	Mrs. Bouncer! Mrs. Bouncer! *(MRS. BOUNCER runs in.)*
MRS. B.:	What is it, gentlemen?
BOX:	Pistols for two!
MRS. B.:	Yes, sir. *(Going)*
COX:	Stop! You don't mean to say, thoughtless and imprudent woman, that you keep loaded firearms in the house?
MRS. B.:	Oh, no — they're not loaded.
COX:	Then produce the murderous weapons instantly! *(Exit MRS. BOUNCER.)*
BOX:	I say, sir!

[20]bride-to-be

COX:	Well, sir?
BOX:	What's your opinion of dueling, sir?
COX:	I think it's a barbarous practice, sir.
BOX:	So do I, sir. To be sure, I don't so much object to it when the pistols are not loaded.
COX:	No. I dare say that does make some difference.
BOX:	And yet, sir — on the other hand — doesn't it strike you as rather a waste of time, for two people to keep firing pistols at another, with nothing in 'em?
COX:	No, sir — not more than any other harmless recreation.
BOX:	Hark ye! Why do you object to marrying Penelope Ann?
COX:	Because, as I've observed already, I can't abide her. You'll be very happy with her.
BOX:	Happy? Me! With the consciousness that I have deprived you of such a treasure? No, no, Cox!
COX:	Don't think of me, Box. I shall be sufficiently rewarded by the knowledge of my Box's happiness.
BOX:	Don't be absurd, sir!
COX:	Then don't you be ridiculous, sir!
BOX:	I won't have her!
COX:	I won't have her!
BOX:	I have it! Suppose we draw lots for the lady — eh, Mr. Cox?
COX:	That's fair enough, Mr. Box.
BOX:	Or, what say you to dice?
COX:	With all my heart! *(Eagerly)* Dice, by all means.
BOX:	*(Aside)* That's lucky! Mrs. Bouncer's nephew left a pair here yesterday. He sometimes persuades me to have a throw for a trifle, and as he always throws sixes, I suspect they are good ones. *(Goes to the cupboard and brings out the dice box.)*
COX:	*(Aside)* I've no objection at all to dice. I lost one pound, seventeen and sixpence, at last Barnet Races, to a very gentlemanly looking man, who had a most peculiar knack of throwing sixes; I suspected they were loaded, so I gave him another half-crown, and he gave me the dice. *(Takes dice out of his pocket. Uses lucifer box as substitute for dice box, which is on table.)*
BOX:	Now then, sir!
COX:	I'm ready, sir! *(They seat themselves at opposite sides of the table.)* Will you lead off, sir?
BOX:	As you please, sir. The lowest throw, of course, wins Penelope Ann?
COX:	Of course, sir.

BOX:	Very well, sir!
COX:	Very well, sir!
BOX:	*(Rattling dice and throwing)* Sixes!
COX:	That's not a bad throw of yours, sir. *(Rattling dice, throws.)* Sixes!
BOX:	That's a pretty good one of yours, sir. *(Throws.)* Sixes!
COX:	*(Throws.)* Sixes!
BOX:	Sixes!
COX:	Sixes!
BOX:	Sixes!
COX:	Sixes!
BOX:	Those are not bad dice of yours, sir.
COX:	Yours seem pretty good ones, sir.
BOX:	Suppose we change?
COX:	Very well, sir. *(They change dice.)*
BOX:	*(Throwing)* Sixes!
COX:	Sixes!
BOX:	Sixes!
COX:	Sixes!
BOX:	*(Flings down the dice.)* Pooh! It's perfectly absurd, your going on throwing sixes in this sort of way, sir.
COX:	I shall go on till my luck changes, sir!
BOX:	Let's try something else. I have it! Suppose we toss for Penelope Ann?
COX:	The very thing I was going to propose! *(They each turn aside and take out a handful of money.)*
BOX:	*(Aside, examining money)* Where's my tossing shilling? Here it is! *(Selecting coin)*
COX:	*(Aside, examining money)* Where's my lucky sixpence? I've got it!
BOX:	Now then, sir, heads win?
COX:	Or tails lose, whichever you prefer.
BOX:	It's the same to me, sir.
COX:	Very well, sir. Heads, I win, tails, you lose.
BOX:	Yes. *(Suddenly)* No. Heads win, sir.
COX:	Very well, go on! *(They are standing opposite of each other.)*
BOX:	*(Tossing)* Heads!

COX:	*(Tossing)* **Heads!**
BOX:	*(Tossing)* **Heads!**
COX:	*(Tossing)* **Heads!**
BOX:	**Ain't you rather tired of turning up heads, sir!**
COX:	**Couldn't you vary the monotony of our proceedings by an occasional tail, sir?**
BOX:	*(Tossing)* **Heads!**
COX:	*(Tossing)* **Heads!**
BOX:	**Heads? Stop, sir! Will you permit me?** *(Taking COX's sixpence)* **Holloa! Your sixpence has got no tail, sir!**
COX:	*(Seizing BOX's shilling)* **And your shilling has got two heads, sir!**
BOX:	**Cheat!**
COX:	**Swindler!** *(They are about to rush upon each other, then retreat to some distance and commence sparring and striking fiercely at one another. Enter MRS. BOUNCER.)*
BOX and COX:	**Is the little back second floor room ready?**
MRS. B.:	**Not quite, gentlemen. I can't find the pistols, but I have brought you a letter. It came by the General Post yesterday. I'm sure I don't know how I forgot it, for I put it carefully in my pocket.**
COX:	**And you've kept it carefully in your pocket ever since?**
MRS. B.:	**Yes, sir. I hope you'll forgive me, sir.** *(Going)* **By the bye, I paid twopence for it.**
COX:	**Did you? Then I do forgive you.** *(Exit MRS. B. COX looks at letter.)* **"Margate." The postmark decidedly says "Margate."**
BOX:	**Oh, doubtless a tender epistle from Penelope Ann.**
COX:	**Then read it, sir.** *(Handing letter to BOX.)*
BOX:	**Me, sir?**
COX:	**Of course. You don't suppose I'm going to read a letter from your intended?**
BOX:	**My intended! Pooh! It's addressed to you — C. O. X!**
COX:	**Do you think that's a C? It looks to me like a B.**
BOX:	**Nonsense! Fracture the seal!**
COX:	*(Opens letter. Starts reading.)* **Goodness gracious!**
BOX:	*(Snatching letter, reads.)* **Gracious goodness!**
COX:	*(Taking letter again)* **"Margate — May the 4th. Sir — I hasten to convey to you the intelligence of a melancholy[21] accident, which has bereft you[22] of your intended wife. He means your intended!**
BOX:	**No, yours! However, it's perfectly immaterial — but she unquestionably was yours.**

[21]sad
[22]left you without

COX:	How can that be? You proposed to her first!
BOX:	Yes, but then you — now don't let us begin again — Go on.
COX:	*(Resuming letter)* "Poor Mrs. Wiggins went out for a short excursion in a sailing boat — a sudden and violent squall soon after took place, which, it is supposed, upset her, as she was found, two days afterwards, keel upwards."
BOX:	Poor woman!
COX:	The boat, sir! *(Reading)* "As her man of business, I immediately proceeded to examine her papers, amongst which I soon discovered her will; the following extract from which will, I have no doubt, be satisfactory to you. 'I hereby bequeath my entire property to my intended husband.' " Excellent, but unhappy creature! *(Affected)*
BOX:	Generous, ill-fated being! *(Affected)*
COX:	And to think that I tossed up for such a woman!
BOX:	When I remember that I staked such a treasure on the hazard of a die!
COX:	I'm sure, Mr. Box, I can't sufficiently thank you for your sympathy.
BOX:	And I'm sure, Mr. Cox, you couldn't feel more if she had been your own intended.
COX:	If she'd been my own intended? She was my own intended!
BOX:	Your intended? Come, I like that! Didn't you very properly observe just now, sir, that I proposed to her first?
COX:	To which you very sensibly replied that you'd come to an untimely end.
BOX:	I deny it!
COX:	I say you have!
BOX:	The fortune's mine!
COX:	Mine!
BOX:	I'll have it!
COX:	So will I!
BOX:	I'll go to law!
COX:	So will I!
BOX:	Stop! A thought strikes me. Instead of going to law about the property, suppose we divide it?
COX:	Equally?
BOX:	Equally. I'll take two-thirds.
COX:	That's fair enough — and I'll take three-fourths.
BOX:	That won't do. Half and half!
COX:	Agreed! There's my hand upon it.

BOX:	And mine. *(As they are about to shake hands, a postman's knock is heard at the street door.)*
COX:	Holloa! Postman again!
BOX:	Postman yesterday — postman today. *(Enter MRS. BOUNCER.)*
MRS. B.:	Another letter, Mr. Cox — twopence more!
COX:	I forgive you again! *(Takes the letter and closes door on MRS. BOUNCER.)* Another trifle from Margate. *(Opens the letter. Starts reading.)* Goodness gracious!
BOX:	*(Snatching letter, reads.)* Gracious goodness!
COX:	*(Snatching letter again — reads.)* "Happy to inform you — false alarm..."
BOX:	*(Overlooking)* "Sudden squall — boat upset — Mrs. Wiggins, your intended..."
COX:	"Picked up by a steamboat..."
BOX:	"Carried into Boulogne..."
COX:	"Returned here this morning..."
BOX:	"Will start by early train, tomorrow..."
COX:	"And be with you at ten o'clock, exact." *(Both simultaneously pull out their watches.)*
BOX:	Cox, I congratulate you!
COX:	Box, I give you joy!
BOX:	I'm sorry that most important business of the Colonial Office will prevent my witnessing the truly happy meeting between you and your intended. Good morning! *(Going)*
COX:	*(Stopping him)* It's obviously for me to retire. Not for worlds would I disturb the rapturous meeting between you and your intended. Good morning!
BOX:	You'll excuse me, sir, but our last arrangement was that she was your intended.
COX:	No, yours!
BOX:	Yours!
BOX and COX:	Yours! *(Ten o'clock strikes — noise Off-stage.)*
COX:	Ha! What's that? A cab's drawn up at the door! *(Running to window)* No — it's a twopenny omnibus![23]
BOX:	*(Leaning over COX's shoulder)* A lady's got out — There's no mistaking that majestic person — it's Penelope Ann!
COX:	Your intended!
BOX:	Yours!
COX:	Yours. *(Both run to door and eagerly listen.)*
BOX:	Hark! She's coming upstairs!

[23]public bus

COX:	**Shut the door!** *(They slam the door, and both lean up against it with their backs.)*
MRS. B.:	*(Without, and knocking)* **Mr. Cox! Mr. Cox!**
COX:	*(Shouting)* **I've just stepped out!**
BOX:	**So have I!**
MRS. B.:	**Mr. Cox!** *(Pushing at the door. COX and BOX redouble their efforts to keep their door shut.)* **Open the door. It's only me, Mrs. Bouncer!**
COX:	**Only you? Then where's the lady?**
MRS. B.	**Gone!**
COX:	**Upon your honor?**
BOX:	**As a gentleman?**
MRS. B.:	**Yes, and she's left a note for Mr. Cox.**
COX:	**Give it to me!**
MRS. B.:	**Then open the door!**
COX:	**Put it under!** *(Letter is put under the door; COX picks up the letter and opens it.)* **Goodness gracious!**
BOX:	*(Snatching letter)* **Gracious goodness!** *(COX snatches the letter, and runs forward, followed by BOX.)*
COX:	*(Reading)* **"Dear Mr. Cox, pardon my candor..."**
BOX:	*(Looking over COX's shoulder and reading)* **"But being convinced that our feelings, like our ages do not reciprocate**[24]**..."**
COX:	**"I hasten to apprise you of my immediate union..."**
BOX:	**"With Mr. Knox!"**
COX:	**Huzza!**
BOX:	**Three cheers for Knox! Ha, ha, ha!** *(Tosses the letter in the air. Begins dancing. COX also dances.)*
MRS. B.:	*(Putting her head in at door)* **The little second floor back room is quite ready!**
COX:	**I don't want it!**
BOX:	**No more do I!**
COX:	**What shall part us?**
BOX:	**What shall tear us asunder?**
COX:	**Box!**
BOX:	**Cox!** *(About to embrace, BOX stops, seizes COX's hand, and looks eagerly in his face.)* **You'll excuse the apparent insanity of the remark, but the more I gaze on your features, the more I'm convinced that you're my long-lost brother.**
COX:	**The very observation I was going to make to you!**

[24]are not similar

BOX:	Ah, tell me — in mercy tell me — have you such a thing as a strawberry mark on your left arm?
COX:	No!
BOX:	Then it is he! *(They rush into each other's arms.)*
COX:	Of course we stop where we are!
BOX:	Of course!
COX:	For, between you and me, I'm rather partial to this house.
BOX:	So am I — I begin to feel quite at home in it.
COX:	Everything so clean and comfortable.
BOX:	And I'm sure the mistress of it, from what I have seen of her, is very anxious to please.
COX:	So she is — and I vote, Box, that we stick by her.
BOX:	Agreed! There's my hand upon it. Join but yours — agree that the house is big enough to hold us both. Then Box —
COX:	And Cox —
BOX and COX:	Are satisfied!

(The curtain falls.)

ABOUT THE AUTHORS

Alan Engelsman received his undergraduate degree in theatre arts from Amherst College and his master's degree from Syracuse University. Since then he has directed and performed in plays, and designed scenery for community theatres, summer stock, and children's theatre. Most importantly, he has been a high school theatre teacher for over thirty years.

Mr. Engelsman authored the first edition *Theatre Arts 1 Student Handbook* and the *Theatre Arts 1 Student Source Book*. In addition, he created the *Theatre Arts 1 Engelsman Theatre Game Cards*. Co-author of *STORYBOARD: The Playwriting Kit* and co-author of two other drama texts, Engelsman has also served as editor of *The Secondary School Theatre Journal*. He has been faculty sponsor of Thespian Troupe 322 at Clayton High School in Suburban St. Louis and an active member of the American Alliance for Theatre and Education.

Penny Engelsman received her undergraduate degree from Washington University and her master's degree from St. Louis University. An educator for over twenty-five years, she has taught at St. Louis Community College since 1972. Ms. Engelsman has written two textbooks, *Writing Lab: A Program That Works* and *Begin Here*, a composition text. In addition, she co-authored *STORYBOARD: The Playwriting Kit* and the 1997 edition of the *Theatre Arts 1 Student Handbook* and the *Theatre Arts 1 Teacher's Course Guide*. Engelsman also has authored three competency skills workbooks for middle and upper grades. Her involvement with community theatre, professional theatre organizations, and high school theatre productions has spanned three decades.

Order Form

Meriwether Publishing Ltd.
P.O. Box 7710
Colorado Springs, CO 80933
Phone: (719) 594-4422
Website: www.meriwetherpublishing.com

Please send me the following books:

_____ **Theatre Arts 2 Student Handbook #BK-B216**   **$22.95**
      by Alan and Penny Engelsman
      On-stage and off stage roles: fitting the pieces together

_____ **Theatre Arts 2 Teacher's Course Guide #BK-B218**   **$24.95**
      by Alan and Penny Engelsman
      Teacher's guide to Theatre Arts 2

_____ **Theatre Arts 1 Student Handbook #BK-B208**   **$19.95**
      by Alan and Penny Engelsman
      A complete introductory theatre course

_____ **Theatre Arts 1 Teacher's Course Guide #BK-B210**   **$24.95**
      by Alan and Penny Engelsman
      Teacher's guide to Theatre Arts 1

These and other fine Meriwether Publishing books are available at your local bookstore or direct from the publisher. Use the handy order form on this page.

Name: _____

Organization name: _____

Address: _____

City: _____ State: _____

Zip: _____ Phone: _____

❑ **Check enclosed**
❑ **Visa/MasterCard/Discover #** _____

                              Expiration
Signature: _____ *Date:* _____
      (required for credit card orders)

Colorado residents: Please add 3% sales tax.
Shipping: Include $2.75 for the first book and 50¢ for each additional book ordered.

❑ *Please send me a copy of your complete catalog of books and plays.*